MICHAËL BORREMANS
FIRE FROM THE SUN

Fire from the Sun, 2017
Oil on panel
10 ⅜ × 11 ⅝ inches
26.4 × 29.5 cm

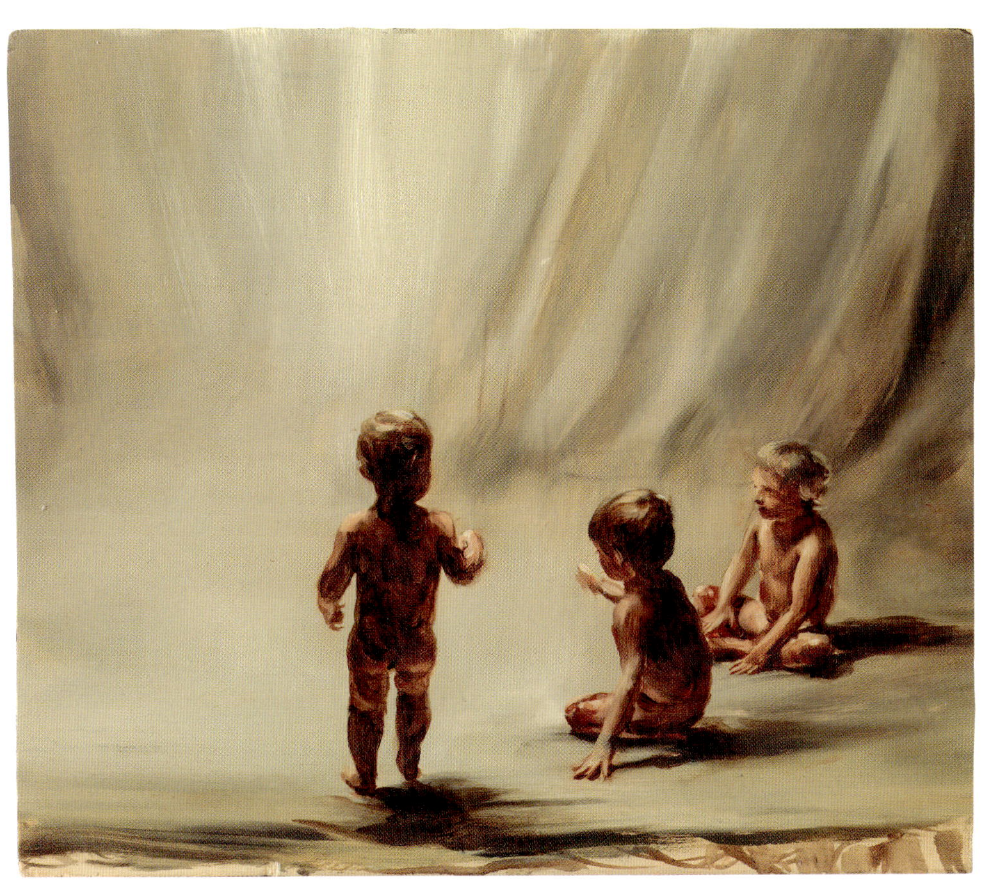

Fire from the Sun, 2017
Oil on panel
8 ¾ × 12 ¼ inches
22.1 × 31 cm

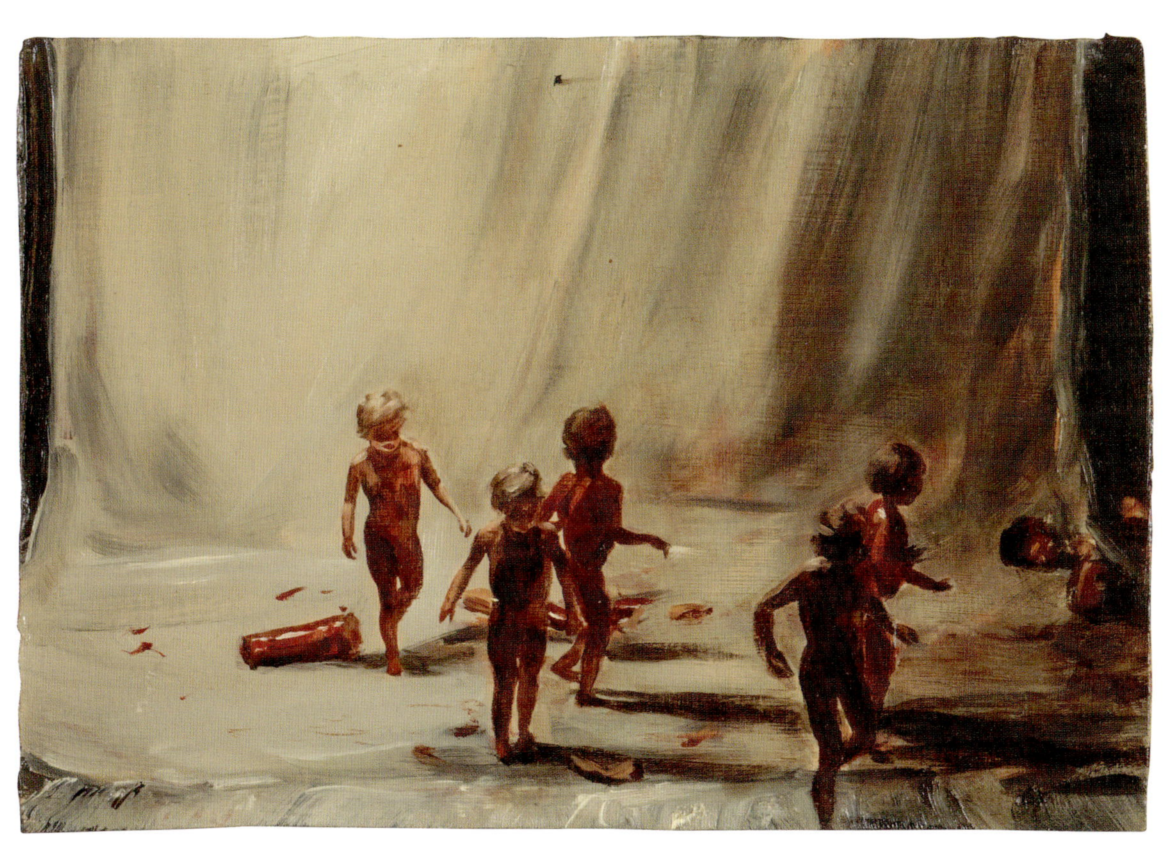

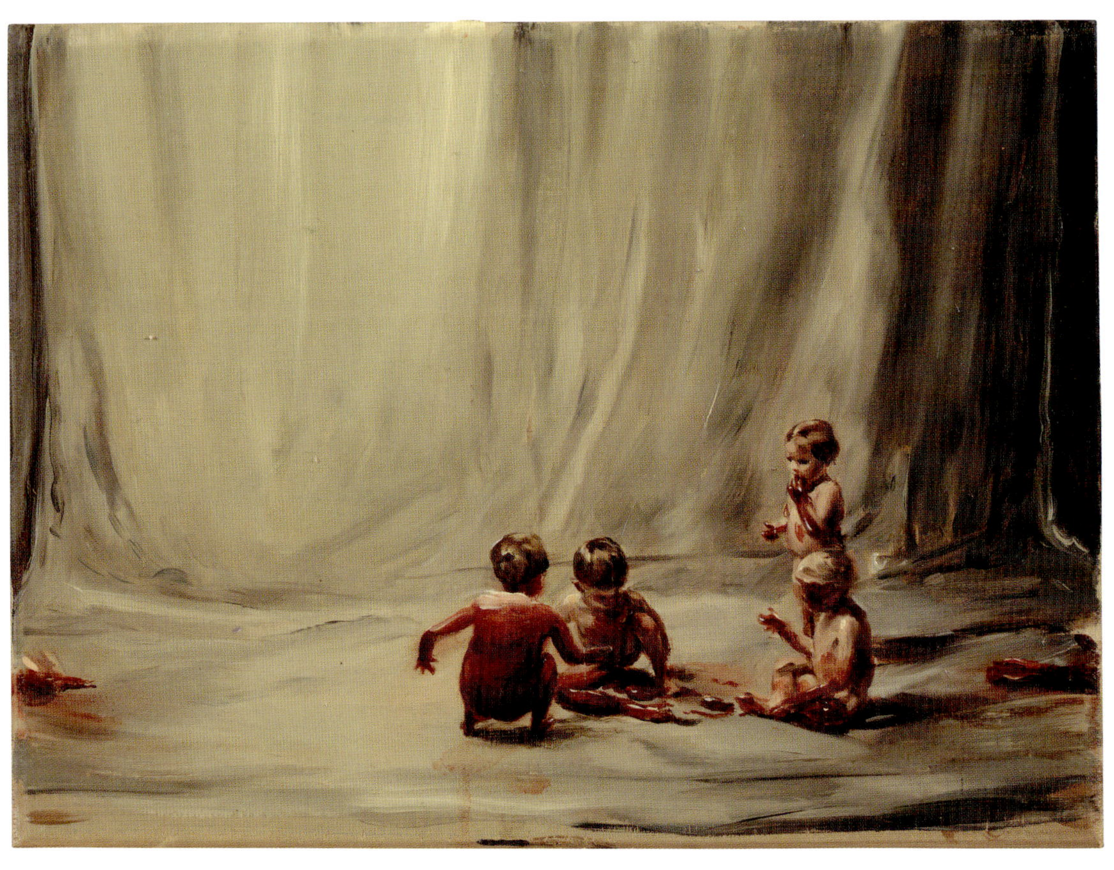

Fire from the Sun, 2017
Oil on panel
10 ¼ × 13 ⅜ inches
26.1 × 34 cm

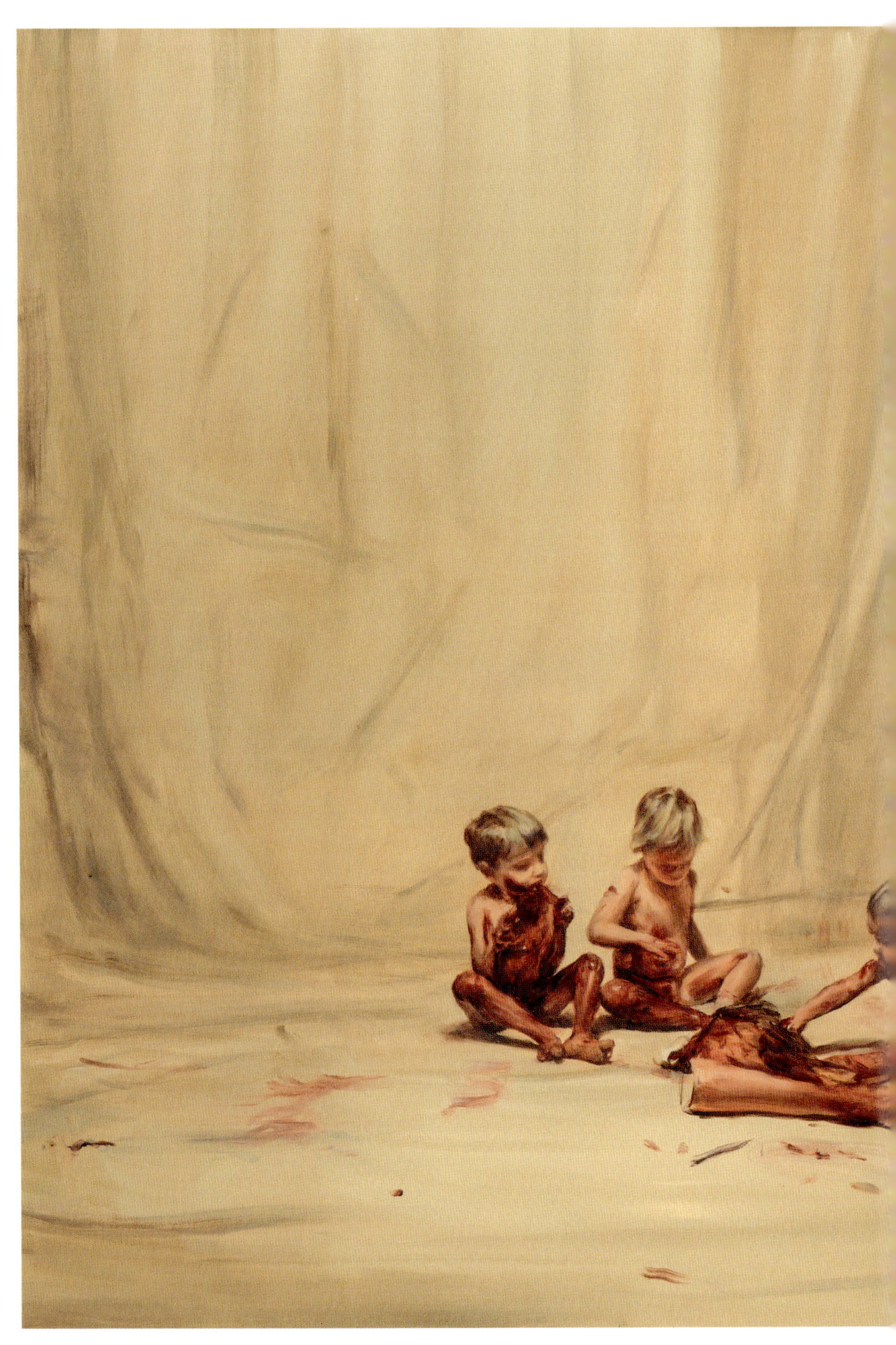

*Fire from the Sun (Three Figures,
One Head, Four Limbs)*, 2017
Oil on canvas
80 ¾ × 110 ¼ inches
205 × 280 cm

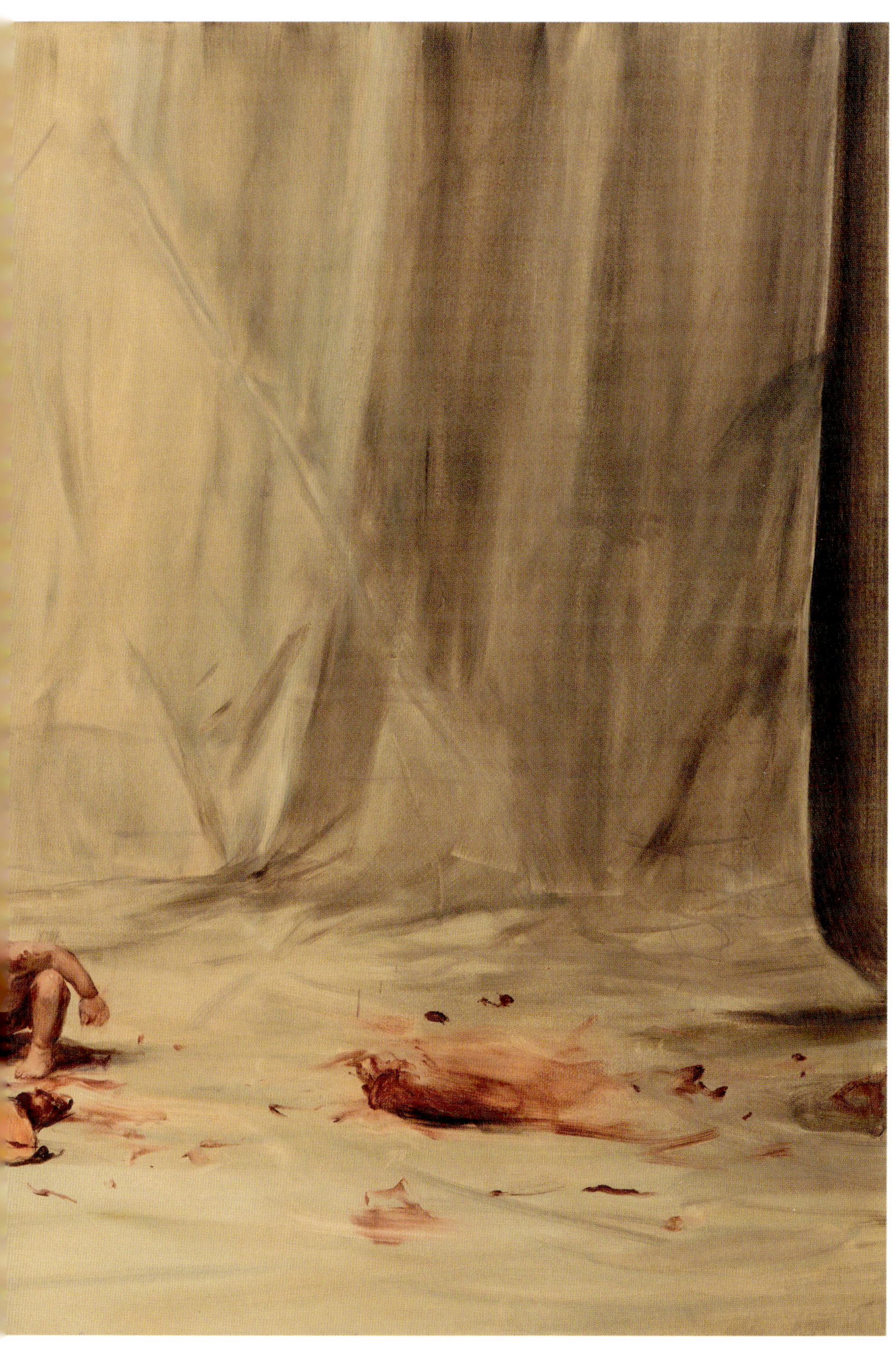

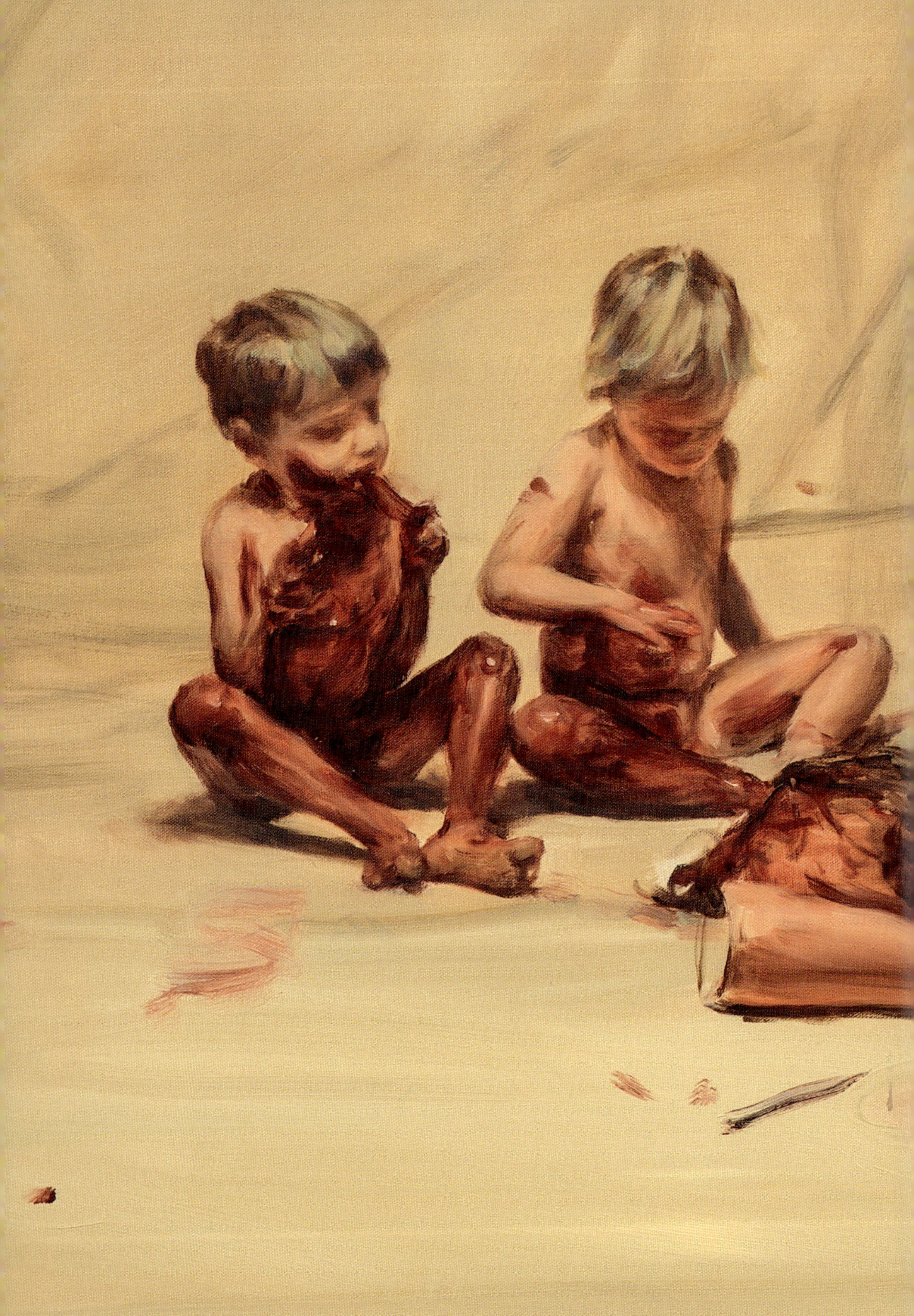

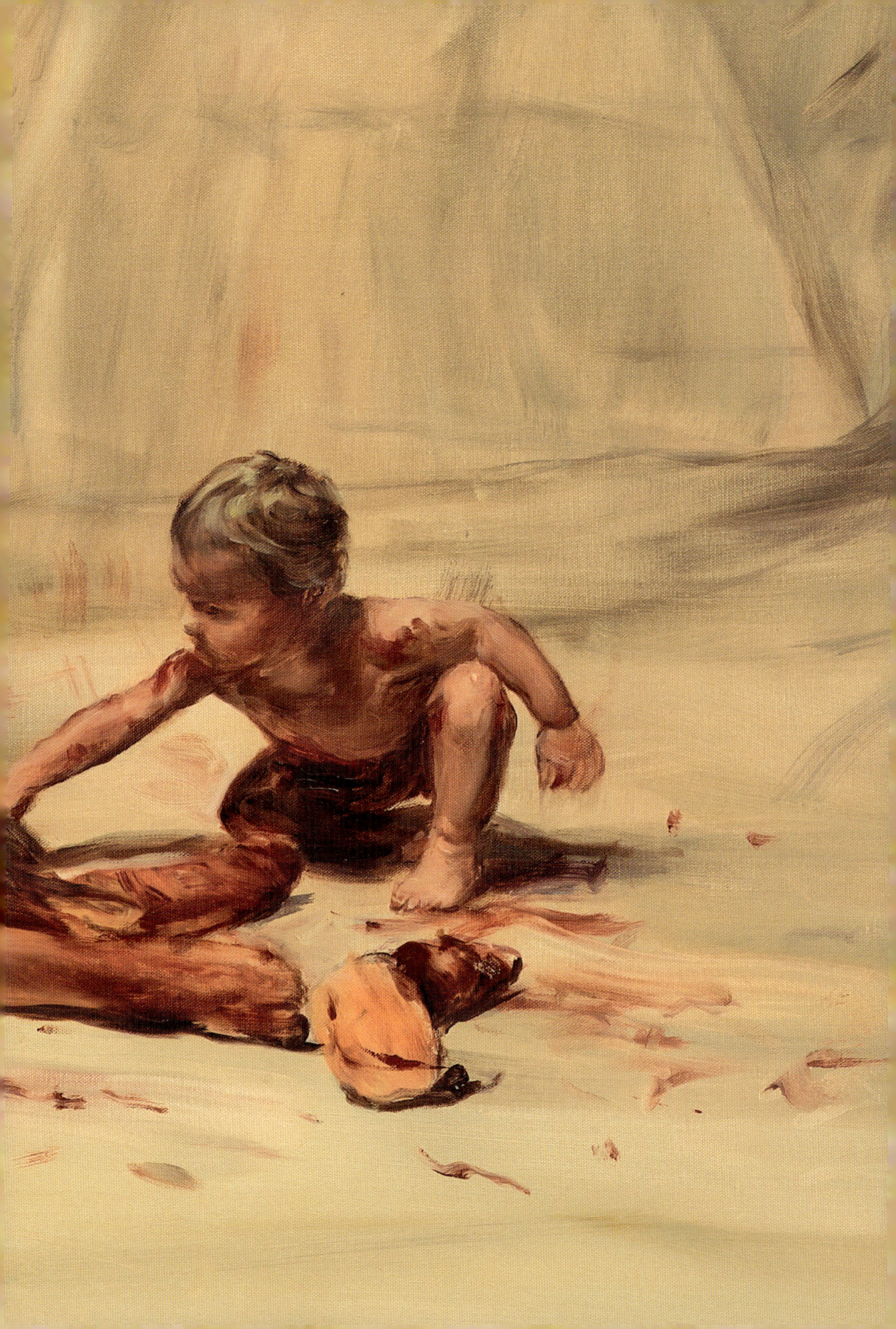

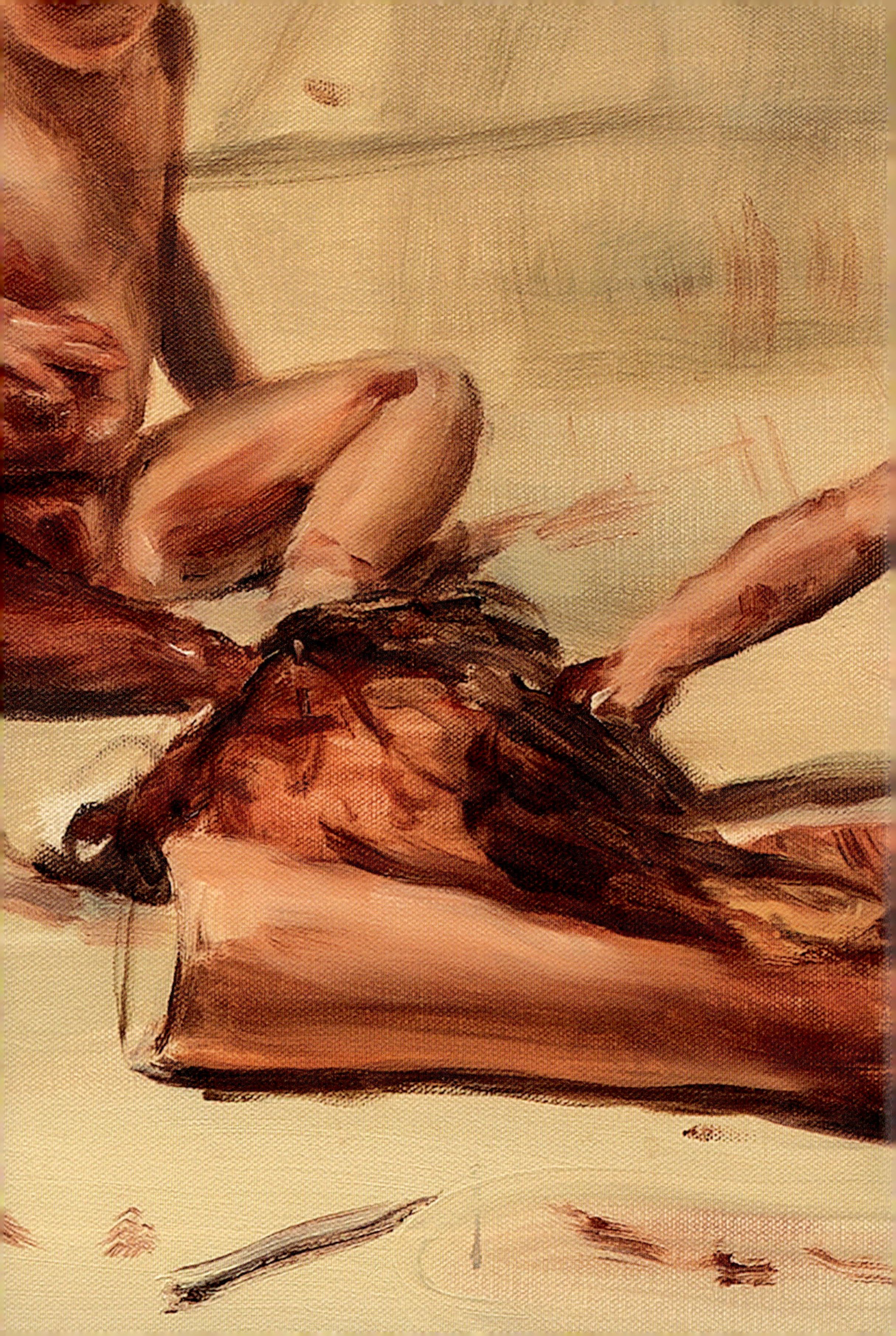

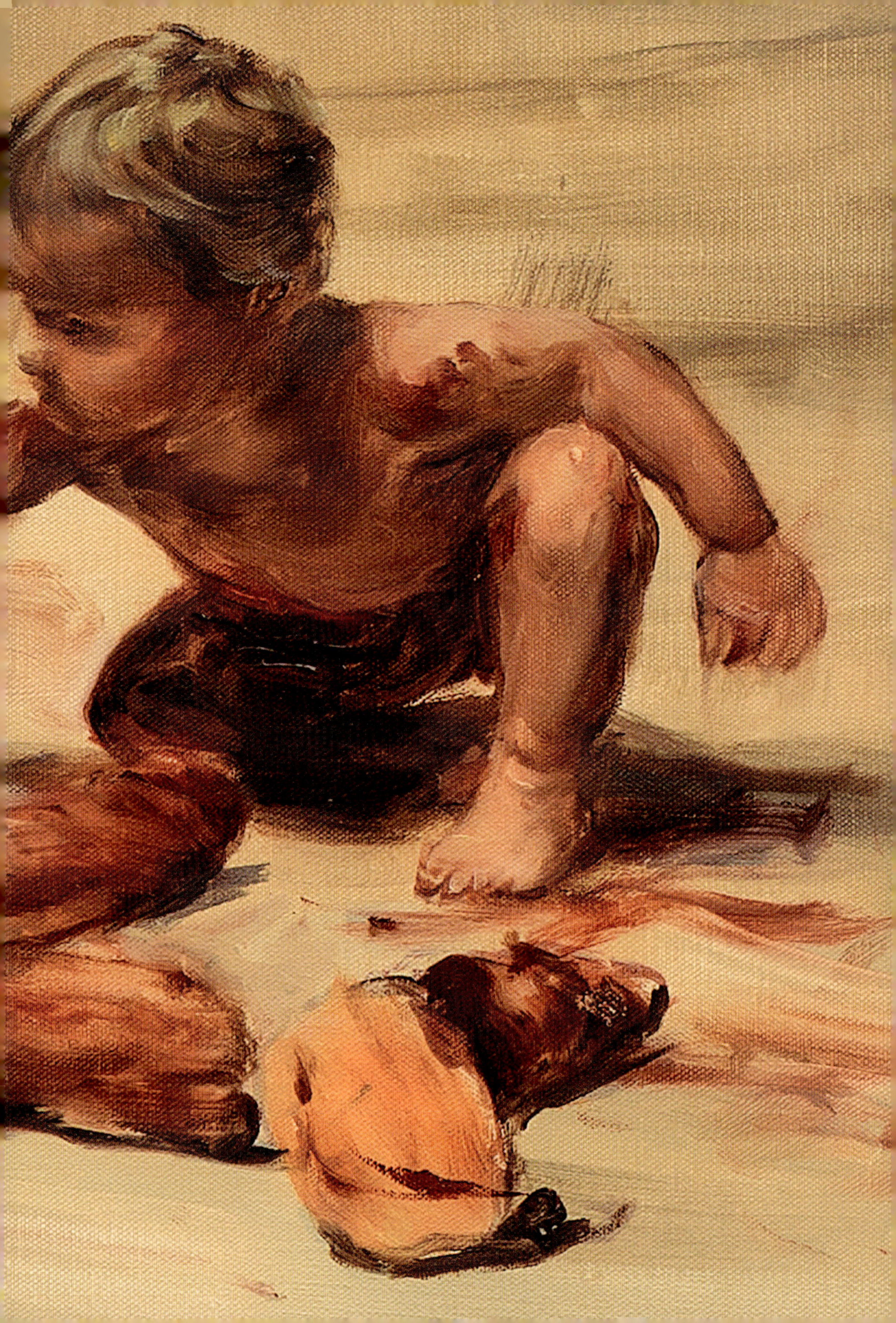

Fire from the Sun, 2017
Oil on cardboard
11 ⅛ × 13 ½ inches
28.2 × 34.2 cm

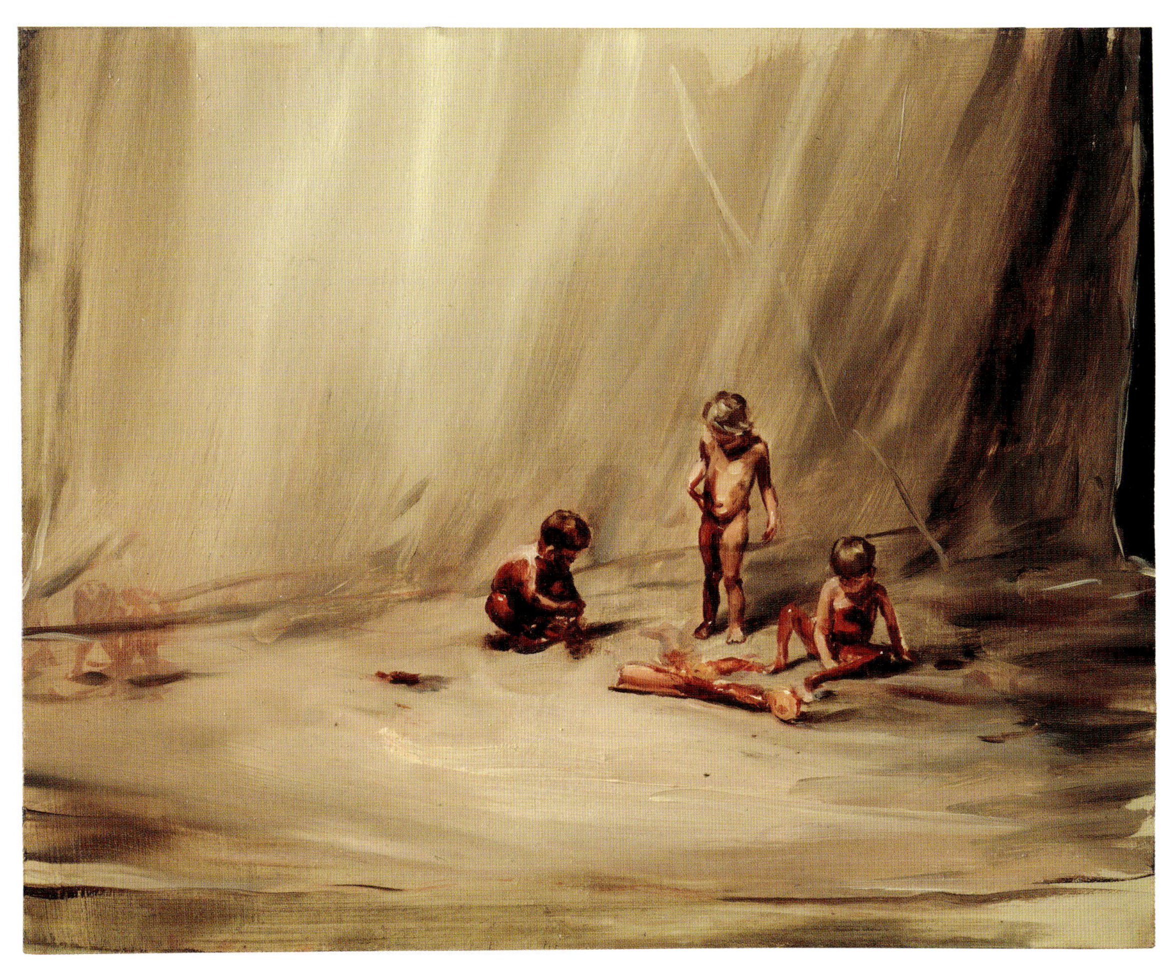

Fire from the Sun, 2017
Oil on canvas
17 × 14 ¼ inches
43 × 36 cm

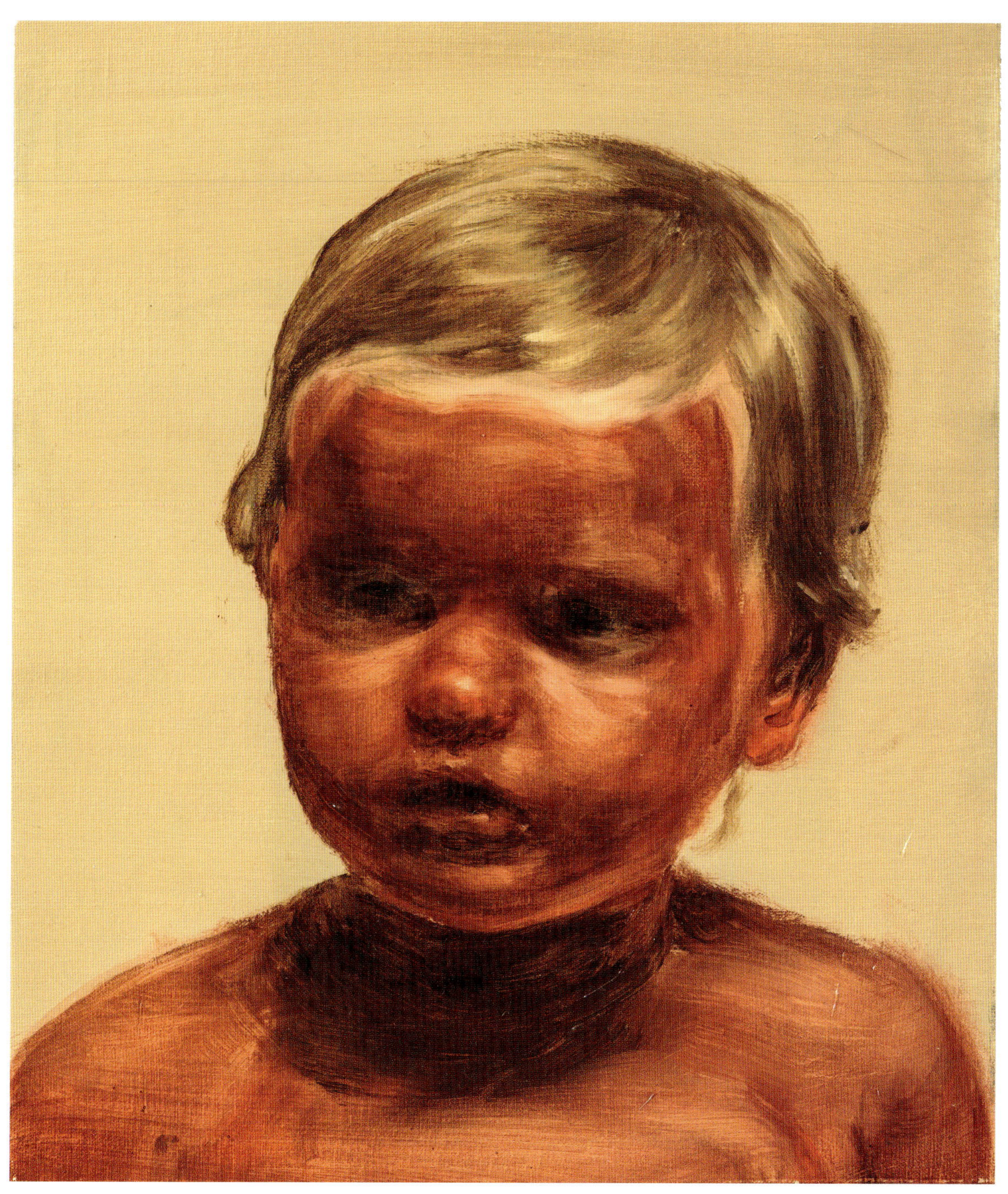

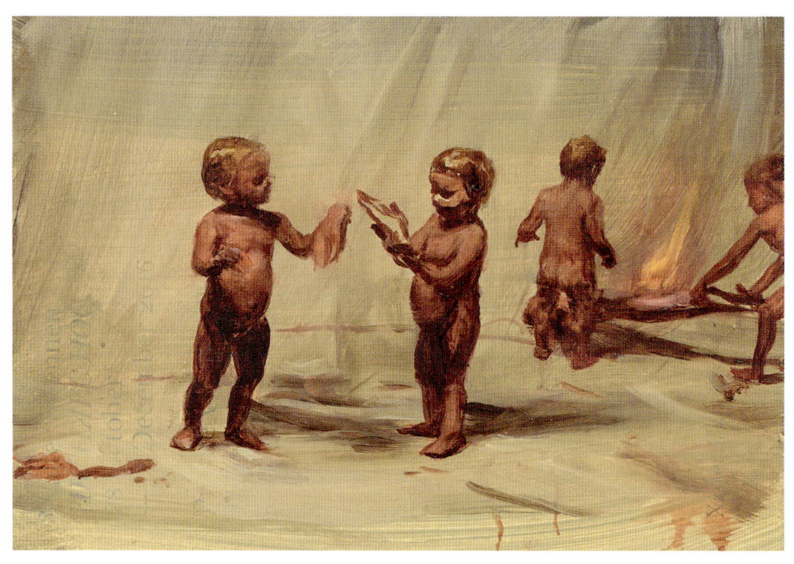

Fire from the Sun, 2017
Oil on cardboard
5 ¾ × 8 ¼ inches
14.5 × 21 cm

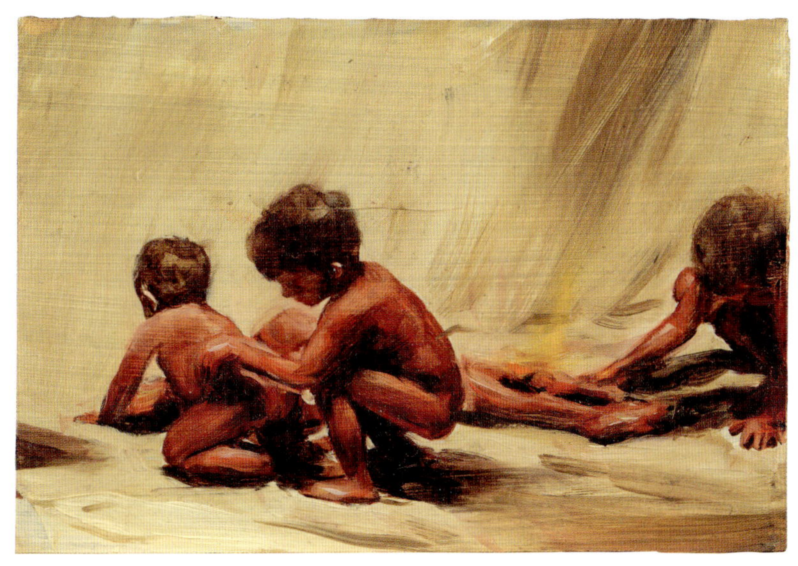

Fire from the Sun, 2017
Oil on cardboard
5 ⅞ × 8 ¼ inches
14.8 × 21 cm

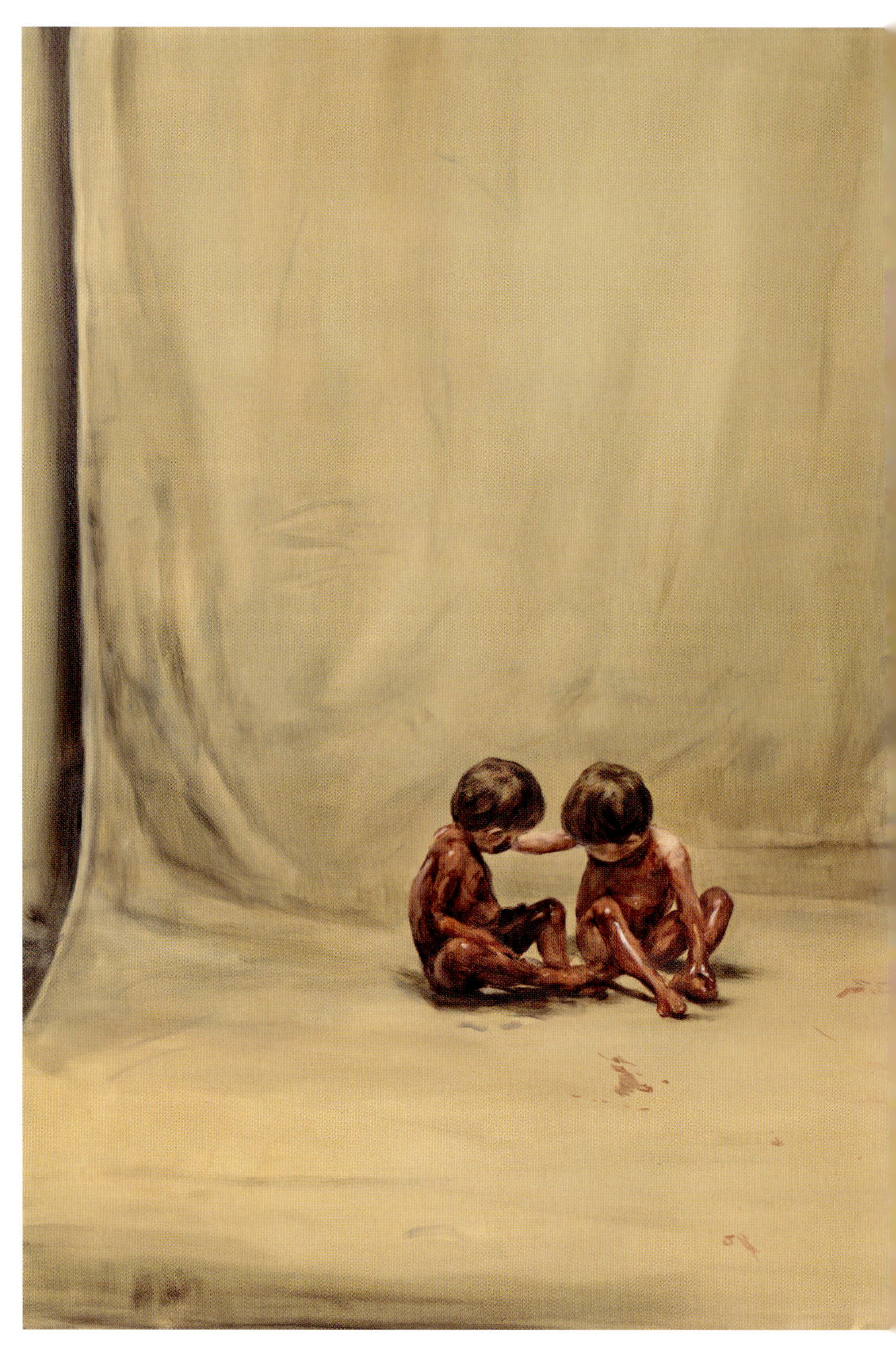

*Fire from the Sun (Three Figures,
Two-and-a-Half Limbs)*, 2017
Oil on canvas
80 ¾ × 110 ¼ inches
205 × 280 cm

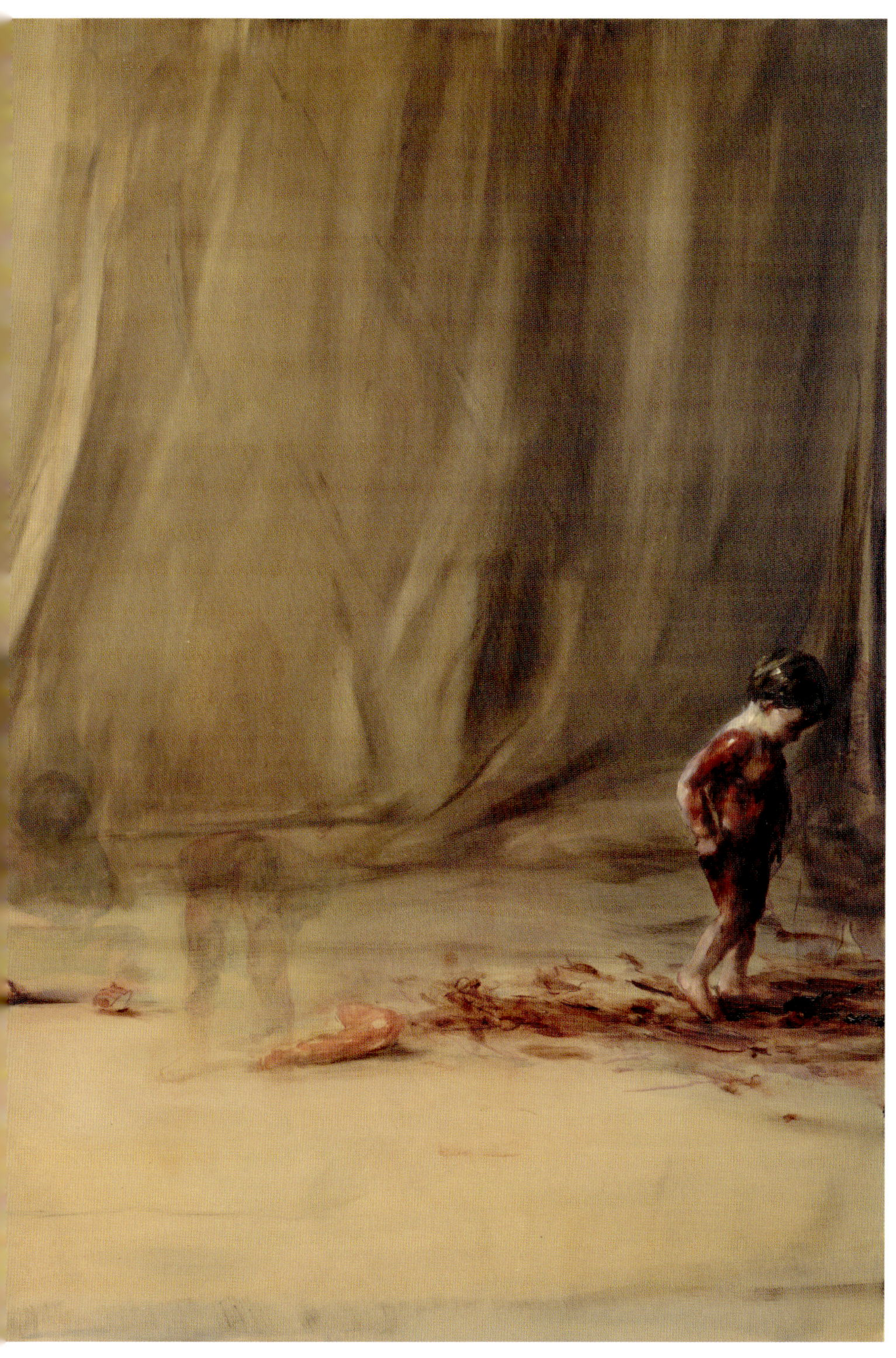

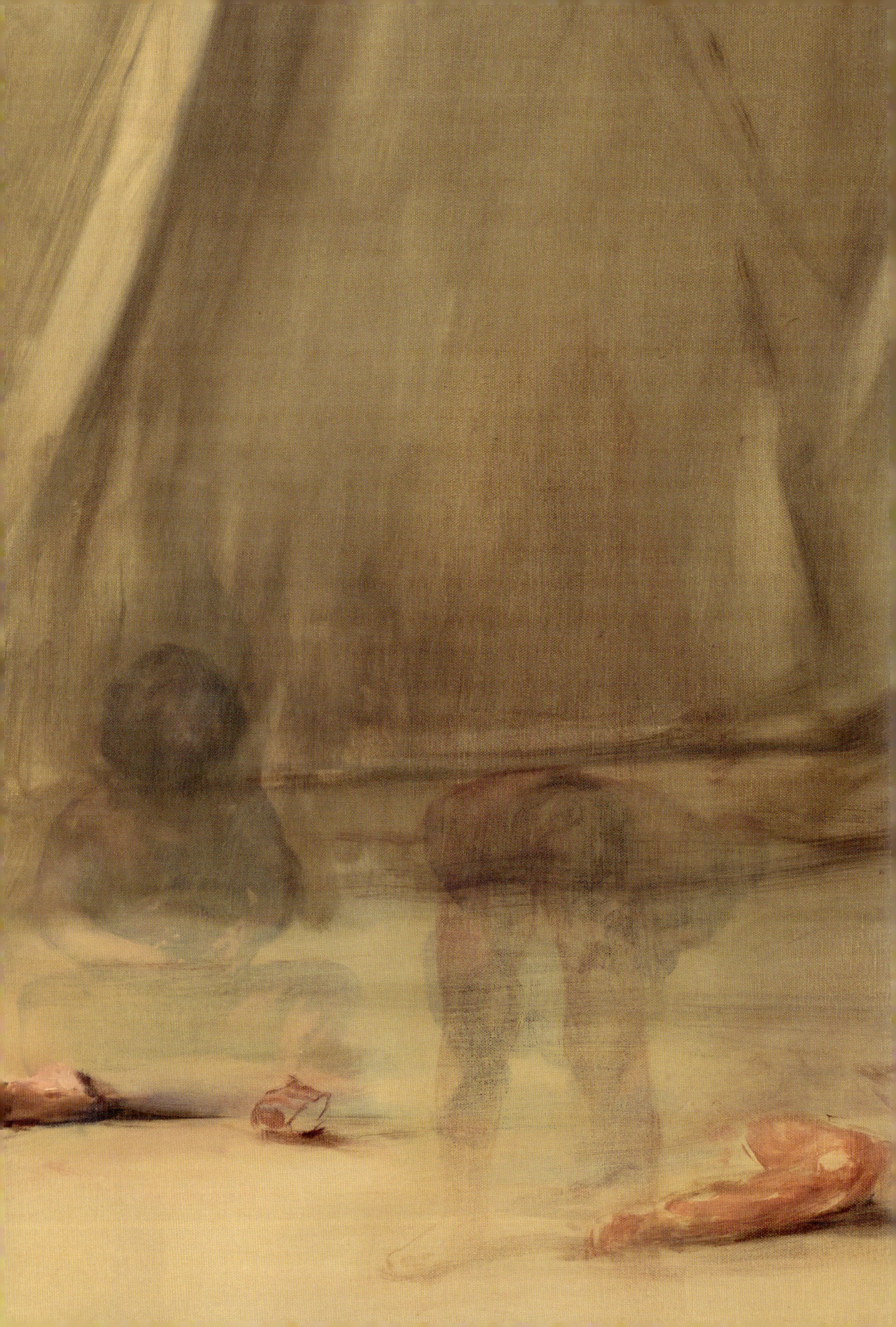

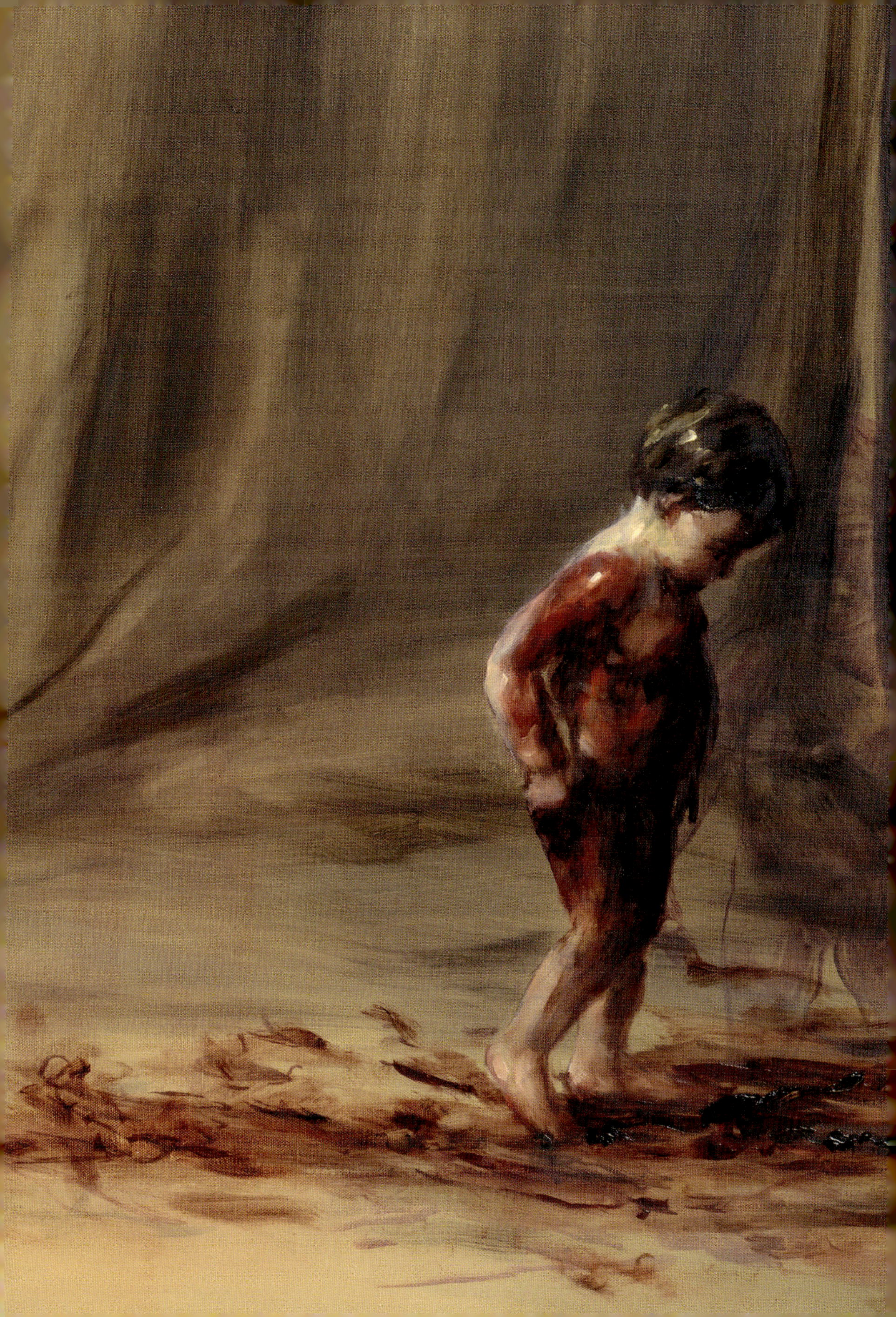

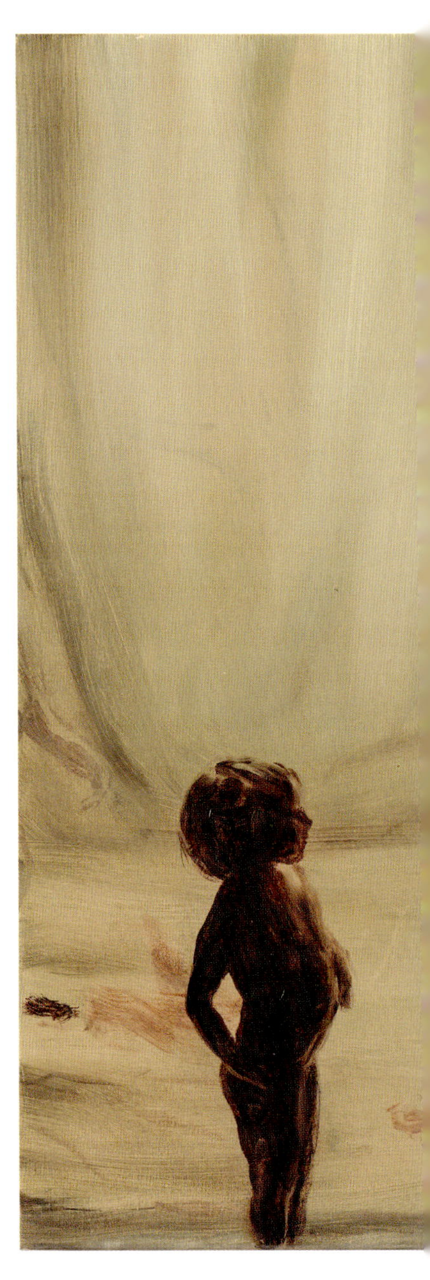

Fire from the Sun
(Three Figures, Three Limbs), 2017
Oil on canvas
31 ½ × 41 ⅜ inches
80 × 105 cm

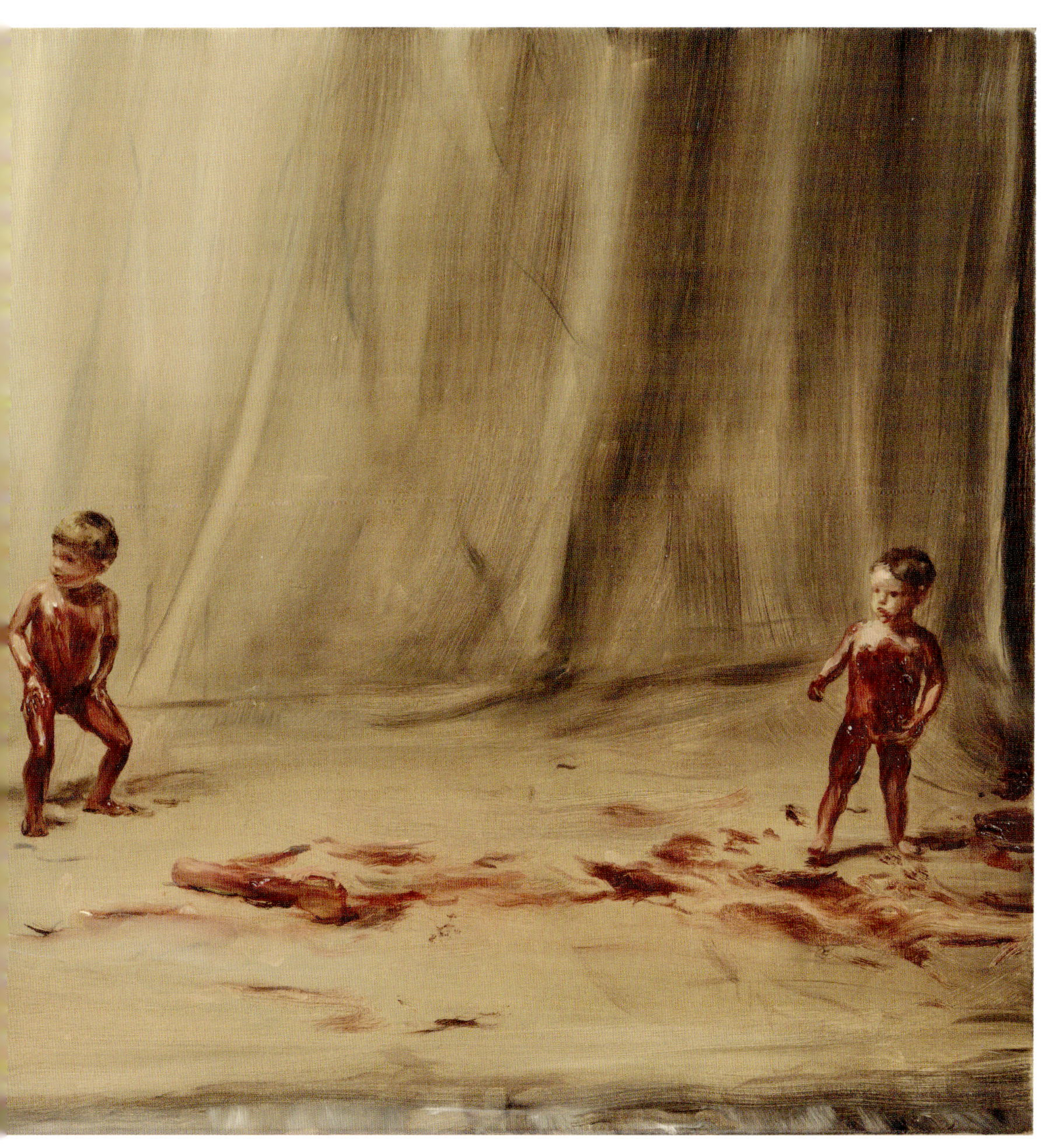

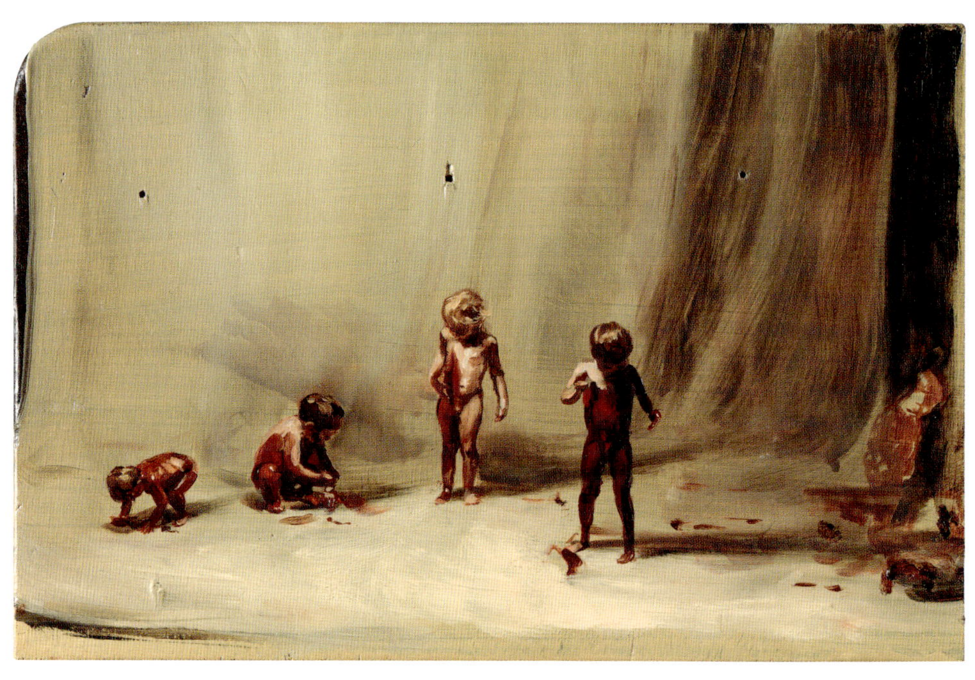

Fire from the Sun, 2017
Oil on panel
8 ⅜ × 12 ¼ inches
21.1 × 31 cm

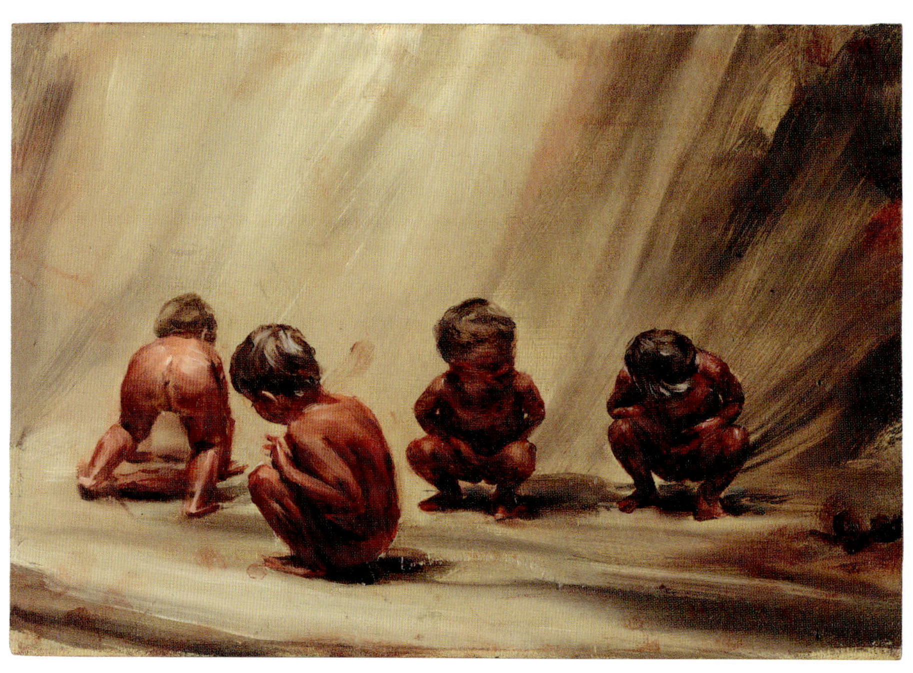

Fire from the Sun, 2017
Oil on panel
9 ⅛ × 12 ⅝ inches
23.1 × 32 cm

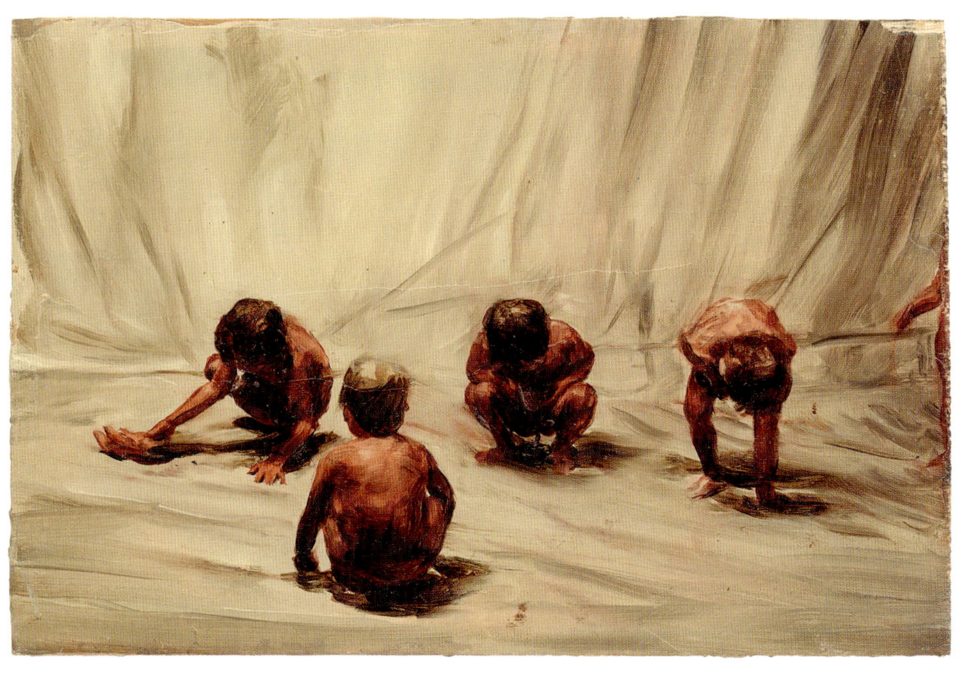

Fire from the Sun, 2017
Oil on panel
8 7⁄8 × 12 7⁄8 inches
22.5 × 32.7 cm

31

Fire from the Sun, 2017
Oil on canvas on cardboard
9 ⅛ × 14 ⅛ inches
23.1 × 35.9 cm

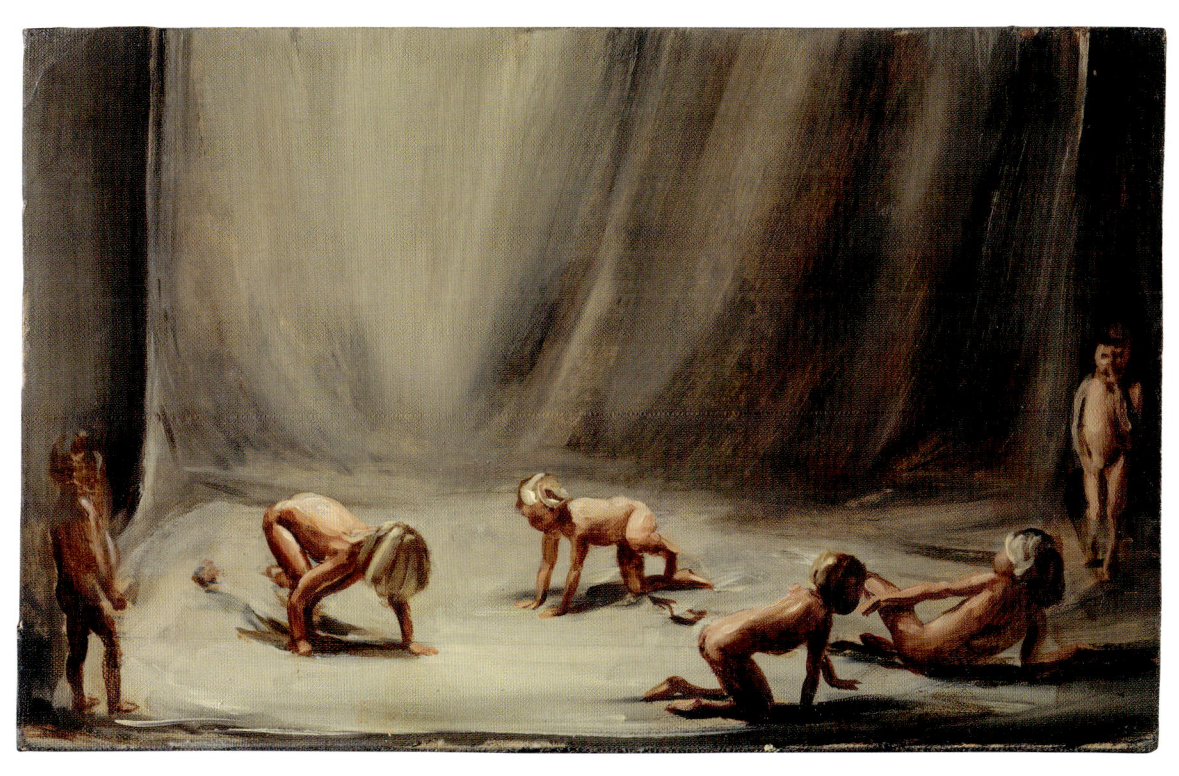

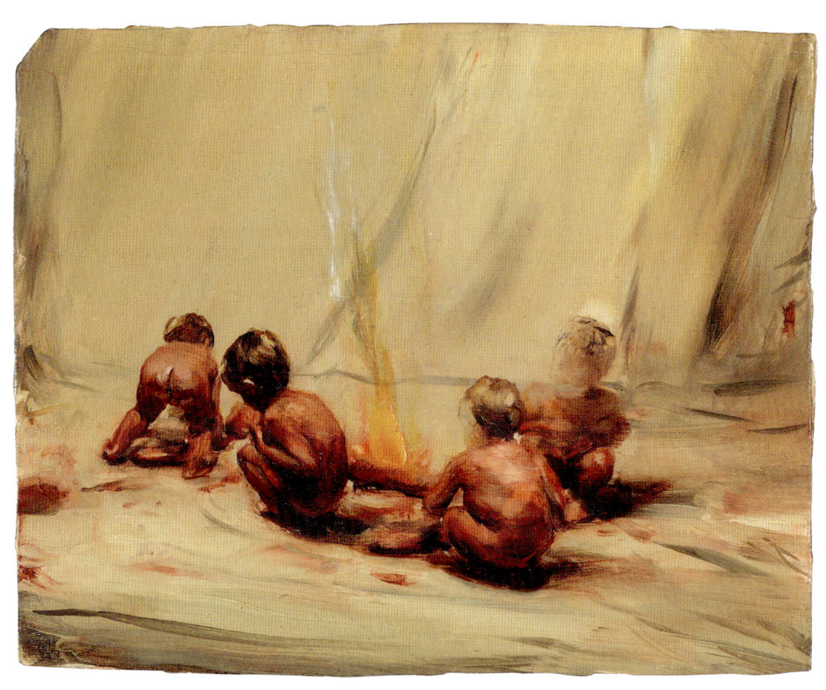

Fire from the Sun, 2017
Oil on panel
8 ⅝ × 10 ⅝ inches
21.7 × 26.9 cm

Michaël Borremans: Fire from the Sun
Michael Bracewell

> Il fait nuit en plein midi…
> —Victor Hugo

On first encounter, the image depicted by the big landscape-format figurative painting is disquieting yet compelling (pp. 10–11). It has an air of gravitas but also of effrontery. It is strange, shocking, enigmatic, teetering on the absurd; it might be derived from myth, or science fiction. In a concise yet complex palette comprising reddish copper, golden brown, scarlet, white gold, and dirty sand, it describes a scene that skews empathetic response.

This is what you get: three naked toddlers—two seated side by side, the other half-crouching, reaching out with one little hand—are playing with what appear to be dismembered and bloody human body parts. The toddlers have golden blond hair, which seems to emphasize their archetypal infancy and innocence. The two seated have the skinny bodies of very young children just out of babyhood; the third, kneeling to reach, looks younger still—slightly pudgy with rolls of baby fat.

They are playing on what seems to be the kind of pull-down paper or fabric backdrop that you would find in a photographer's studio. Sandy brownish ochre in color, the expanse is lit to a golden glow that accentuates the blond hair of the children playing before it and upon it. This golden-ochre paper or fabric is far from pristine: it is creased and slightly sagging like a well-used theater backdrop, and appears to have two tent-like imprints or outlines— one half the size of the other—just visible, like repair seams or indentations in its surface.

To the viewer's right, this backdrop—seemingly raw and coarse in texture, yet theatrically responsive to light— is in slight shadow and flush to a wall. Where it has been pulled forward onto the floor, creating a rather uneven and rumpled foreground, it brings the colors of a children's sandpit to mind.

And then there are the dabs and smears of blood in what appear to be varying degrees of thickness and freshness. Perhaps the little ones have been running amok, as children will. To the viewer's right, for instance, there is what seems to be a particularly gory, dense then spreading bloodstain, congealing to black around its edge. In its diffusion of

reddish-copper-scarlet and intimation of drying stickiness—
the corporeality of blood—this detail might bring to mind
Francis Bacon's painting *Blood on Pavement* (c. 1988): the
transformation of blood into brutish, primal "stuff."

The three children, meanwhile, appear to have reached that
point in their playing when initial exuberance has quietened to
absorbed curiosity. Their activity looks ludic, sensory, utterly
unselfconscious. They are still of an age to be completely
unaware of their nakedness, like infants playing on a beach or
by a swimming pool on a very hot day. Their "messiness"—
their fragile, healthy bodies splattered and covered by what
looks like abundant blood and gore—brings to mind both
the consequences of any toddler game with paints or water,
and more disturbingly, in this seeming context, the Freudian
infant sexual rites of polymorphous perversity.

One little boy's legs and chest are covered with "blood"
as though he had been playing with a bucket of Nutella
chocolate spread; his identically blond companion is similarly
daubed but still has one un-dirtied leg. Have they perhaps
been rubbing themselves, or one another, with whatever this
bloody substance might be?

Any horrified expectations—worst fears—are confirmed
by the gruesome accoutrements to this stark, oddly
stage-lit scene, in which archetypal innocence appears
assaulted and befouled by evidence of slaughter—engrossed
and entertained by that from which it ought to be protected.
For in front of the absorbed trio, the more horrific for
being indistinct, are what seem to be a severed human head
and some amputated limbs. These bloody body parts
have become playthings. The little children's messiness seems
more shocking—if such a thing were possible—for the
blandly accepting way in which they apply themselves (as
infants will) to a game that offers sensory as much as
perceptual fascination.

Such might be a viewer's experience of one of the
paintings by Michaël Borremans that comprise his exhibition
Fire from the Sun. Perhaps these ruddy toddlers are tiny
tongues of flame.

In a body of work made up principally (but not exclusively)
of painting and drawing, dating back to the middle years of
the 1990s, Borremans has explored subjects, forms, and visual
semantics in a manner that is densely atmospheric, seemingly
but not necessarily narrative, and likewise allusive more to the
imagining of art history than to its factual actuality.

The temper and subject matter of his oeuvre of paintings resemble transmissions from a non-specific, crepuscular modernism, yet tinted by an ambience one might reflexively associate with the art of northern European old masters. At the same time, there is a profound aesthetic richness and mysteriousness to his work, a luxuriant sense of texture, warmth, poise, and presence, which seems often subliminally— or overtly—related to intensely romantic eroticism.

The defining characteristic in the art of Michaël Borremans, however, would seem to be its balancing of sensibilities: of precision and ambiguity (itself a device of eroticism), sense and non-sense, representation and the undermining of representation with formalistic or surrealistic swerves of meaning. There is always, more or less, a sense of sinister, threatening, or melancholy twilight in Borremans's art: an atmosphere at once quiet and tense, sexually charged— the rituals of fetish insinuated, but seldom depicted too specifically—and as though located within or drawn from obscure institutional or domestic interiors, shadowy and mostly silent.

These qualities are articulated, made poetically as well as brutally or unnervingly eloquent through the gestural acuity of the painting process, as Borremans seems to bring the sensuality of his subjects to life by imbuing them with a near blurred softness. The viewer feels the mood and body temperature of the figures in these paintings—can sense their repose, remoteness, concentration, or reverie.

Likewise, light, texture, and temperament are given their own particular and peculiar sentience through the abuttal of tonal softness and pictorial concision. The viewer might be reminded, simultaneously, of a cache of old photographs discovered by chance, and the art historical gravitas of painterly values. We are caught in a strange time loop, in which the nobility of execution ascribed to old masters—the re-creation in painting of human presence, caught both stilled, in a particular instant of its being, and for eternity—is placed in the service of vertiginous modernist vision.

What looks like stately darkness or the luminosity of pale spring sunshine is brought by Borremans to the depiction of the uncanny, the perhaps secret, the bizarre, the ordinary inhabited by the otherworldly, and human identity and natural order subjected to strange shifts of form and consciousness. In his paintings, all seems held in the psychological tension between intense painterly values and supernaturally infiltrated quietude: ash-gray twilight; a temperate, modest softness; humankind being almost dutifully human, but weirdly so.

The paintings that comprise *Fire from the Sun* have a new harshness about them, tonally as much as thematically. They appear brutal, agitated. They are nearly all depictions of naked, blond-haired toddlers, their bodies in some instances a demonic red, and in most instances (but not always) seen playing with bloody body parts. In some the children are seen without the gory limbs, either seemingly regarding something the viewer cannot see—perhaps just playing a game—or absorbed in some chaotic group activity. The golden-ochre backdrop is ubiquitous. Some of the paintings are made on large canvases; the majority, somewhat smaller, on panel.

There is also more than an insinuation that these infant games or rites, primal, primitive, or feral activities, include cannibalism—that these blond toddlers accept and engage in the consumption of one another as central to whatever their society might be. The sticky and abundant reddish brown of the blood, the sense of gorging, the absorption of the small children in their activities, the body parts and limbs—all the more gory and violent for being indistinct—all propose the eating of human flesh.

These scenes—in one sense the same bloody episode repeated, in different configurations—both fascinate and appall, in a manner not dissimilar to Goya's celebrated, terrifying and mysterious pictures of both cannibals and cannibalistic old women and witches. Goya's *Dream of a Good Witch* (1819–1823), for example, shows an old woman, bent and leaning on her stick, as she carries on her back a cluster of trussed babies, as though they were a butcher's delivery.

As for Goya, this theme—repellent, visually sadistic— pervades *Fire from the Sun* in a manner that seems at once specific and otherworldly, nightmarish. It seems to serve as both a metaphor for human cruelty and barbarism, individual and collective, and as an insight into the darkest recesses of consciousness. The latter, so commonly manifested historically, wherein the will operates outside of any ethical or moral code, becomes unbounded, capable of anything, determined only on its own satisfaction, however base or psychopathic.

There is also a much smaller group of paintings included within *Fire from the Sun* depicting archaic-looking scientific equipment, the functions of which are unknown and inscrutable. The machines look vaguely mid-twentieth century,

*Man Holding
His Nose*, 2007
Oil on canvas
14 ¼ × 11 ⅞ inches
36 × 30 cm

Automat, 2008
Oil on canvas
31 ½ × 23 ⅝ inches
80 × 60 cm

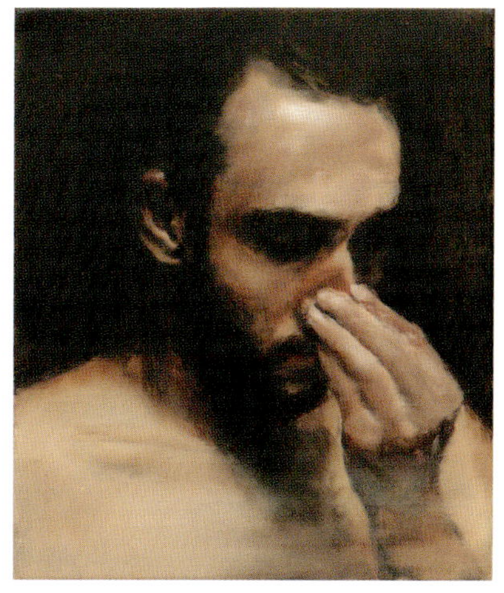

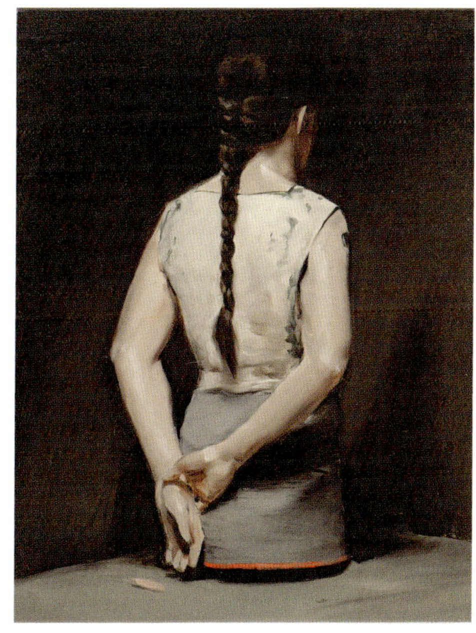

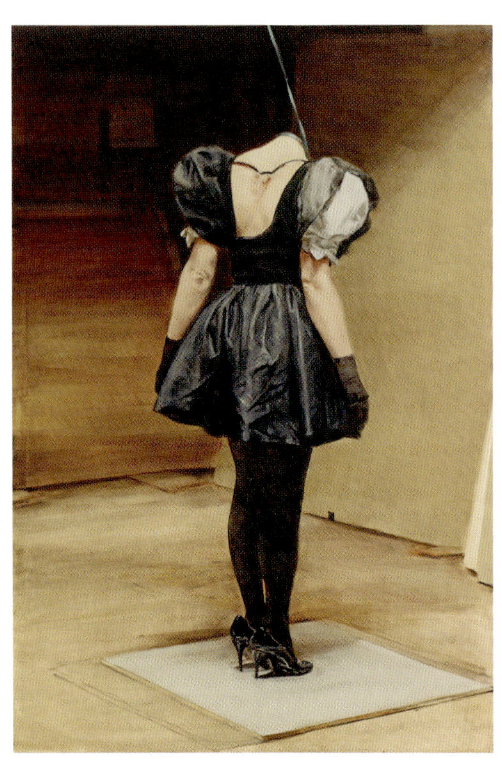

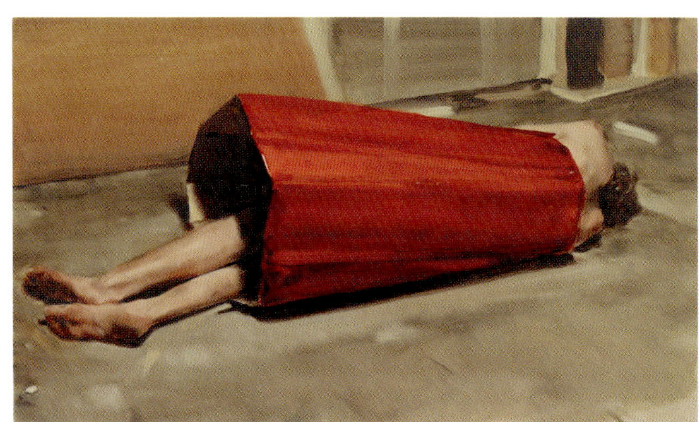

The Loan, 2011
Oil on canvas
122 × 80 ¾ inches
310 × 205 cm

*The Devil's
Dress (II)*, 2011
Oil on canvas
29 ⅜ × 48 ⅞ inches
74.5 × 124 cm

The Limbs, 2016
Oil on canvas
78 ¾ × 47 ¼ inches
200 × 120 cm

The Promise V, 2016
Oil on canvas
12 ⅞ × 10 ⅜ inches
32.5 × 26.2 cm

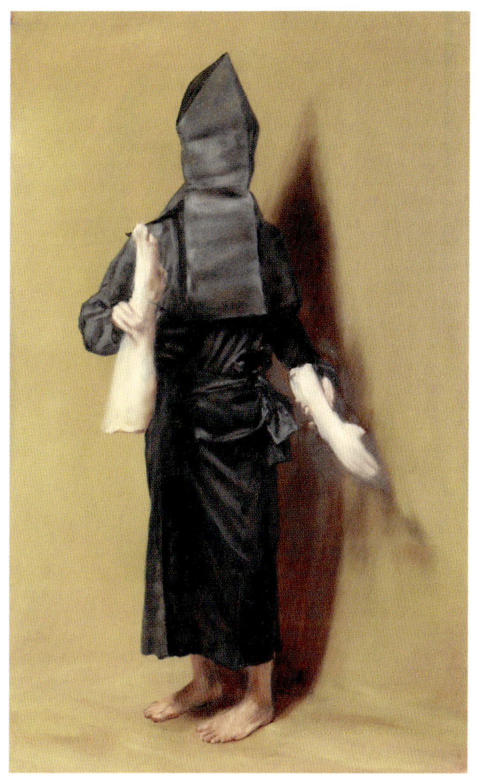

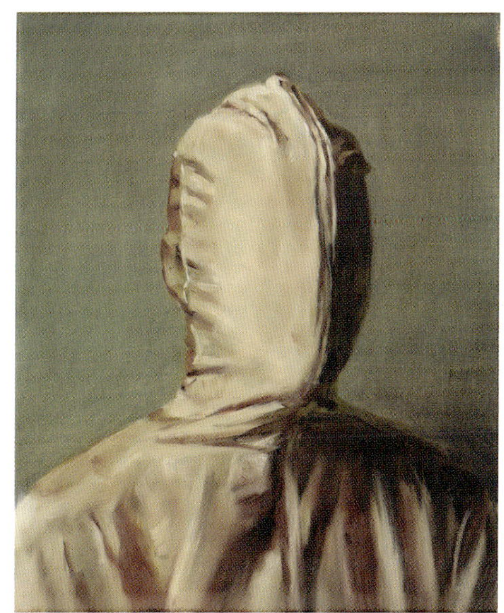

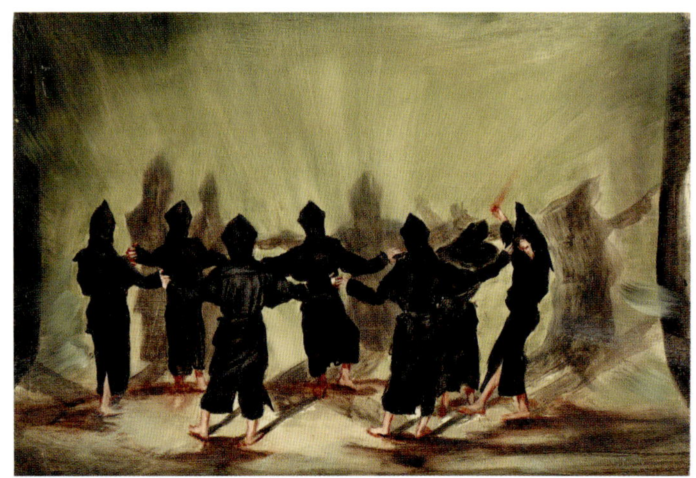

Sirtaki, 2016
Oil on wood
8 ⅞ × 12 ¾ inches
22.5 × 32.4 cm

Mud Boy, 2017
Oil on canvas
16 ⅝ × 14 ¼ inches
42 × 36 cm

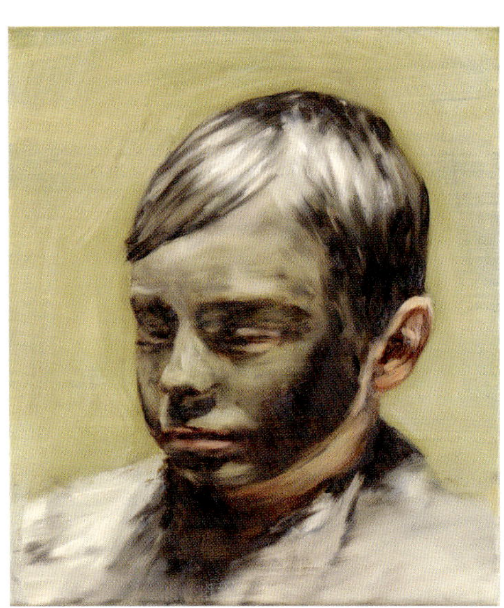

heavy, perhaps related to physics or electrical measurement. The pictorial disjunction between these cold, dormant scientific instruments, and the intent, absorbed, inquiring infants may also create an associative dialogue between them: that the little children and the machines share a sensibility—an aesthetic brutality perhaps, articulating enigma and disquiet.

There is little overt cruelty in the earlier art of Michaël Borremans, but there is much portent. What often look to be innocent figures, obedient to a procedure, to rules or instructions—at times resembling participants in an experiment, at others in what might be sex games— are depicted either alone and posed, or engaged in some vaguely bureaucratic group task. Any tenderness seems always shadowed by coldness. Their activities imply some unclear pursuit, in which science, medical research, sexual fetish, ritual and dream logic seem equally present. Each scene has the strange fusion of ambiguity and precision, peculiar to memorable dreams.

To ascribe specific meanings to the demeanor, identities, and activities of these figures and tableaux would be to misunderstand their nature. Rather, they seem to exist as depictions of psychological states unified perhaps by common themes, but not all of which, by any means, are intended to make "sense." Rather, they exist solely in the world of their strangeness, extremism, and narrative illogicality— in their acute suggestiveness, as opposed to however their meaning might be conjectured. The viewer feels that the attempt to "solve" these paintings could never be more than a stab in the dark.

What these paintings compel, with intense and often unnerving allure, is a visceral sense of empathetic engagement that their subjects simultaneously disrupt or stall with insinuated secondary meanings. It is as though the paintings are magnetizing their strangeness or disquiet to the viewer's sense of spectacle, fantasy, and curiosity; destabilizing pictorial conservatism or artistic "respectability" through intensity of atmosphere, displacements of meaning and unnerving allusion.

Each group of paintings appears to investigate the artistic depiction of a particular activity, gesture, or demeanor, as these might exist as themes, however abstract, mysterious, or illogical. As such these paintings seem to explore aspects of consciousness, as those aspects may exist as incidents from the subconscious, dream world or fantasy—as psychological commentary upon the *primal* nature of otherwise quotidian and commonplace subjects.

The world depicted (or conjured) by the art of Michaël Borremans seems to be an apparently temperate, modest enough realm—a place of academic libraries and soft rain— but also one in which figures are stitched into hooded, full-body suits; or what look like downcast, dreaming adolescents are seen with thickly and brightly painted faces; or where muscular young men, their heads hooded with white fabric, dance or shake topless against a dirty backdrop, holding aloft what look like blurred portions of (human?) meat.

It is likewise a place of crypto-sexual encounter, in which young girls with flawless complexions, neatly and still childishly dressed—sweaters and pleated skirts—stare ahead with clear eyes, obediently assuming poses that both intensify, fetishize, and scrutinize their innocence. No legs visible; skirt hem falling neatly to polished tabletop.

Seen from the back, a young woman's ponytail pulled upwards; likewise from behind, a seemingly headless young woman in black high heels and short black cocktail frock with puff sleeves—a pale blue ribbon ascending from her neck, shadows above and ahead of her. Likewise, a young woman in a gray skirt and sleeveless white top, her long pigtail falling between her shoulder blades to the waistband of her skirt; her hands are behind her back, the right hand holding the left, gently but firmly, as if to take her own pulse...

And then: sleeping men, young men in séance-like circles, suited older men leaning over what look like laboratory benches or office desks, always in gray twilight—photic synonyms for obscurity. A sapling branch leans against an off-white wall. Sleepers and masks and inferences of altered states and institutions; of wounds and of trances; the journey of these paintings feels to be as dark as it is poetic— some inquiry, scientific, or psychical, into the nature of obedience and control.

In this, the bravura of Borremans's painting, the sheer aesthetic accomplishment of its figuration and empathetic power, seems also to be an alibi. His technical accomplishment, supreme conservatism of style and inspired but disciplined formalism, perhaps all serve to empower and cloak their opposite: the arcane or dark psychology of his subject matter and themes—the mysteriousness, moral ambiguity, violence,

portent, somnambulism, brutality, dream logic, allusion,
and insinuation.

Borremans seems to deploy fine artistic historicism as
the agent of Freudian and Jungian themes that are in
turn destabilized, volatile, confrontational, interrogatory.
Painterly acuity, drama, and draughtsmanship, as descended
from a lineage of old and modern masters that might include,
in addition to Goya, Bruegel, Fragonard, Manet, Balthus,
and Magritte—anatomists all of the proximity of stillness and
formality to violence, primal forces, and abandon—serves
in its representational correctitude to empower and intensify
thematic strangeness, provocation, and anarchy.

The paintings comprising *Fire from the Sun* may both
consolidate and advance such an understanding. In every
sense—unsurprisingly—the images of apparently bloodied
naked infants, disporting self-absorbedly amidst cannibalistic
carnage, confront and aggress the viewer's perceptual and
ethical bearings. They do so tonally, pictorially, thematically,
and morally.

And thus we encounter a large, landscape-format
painting, with the same sandy ochre backdrop as before
(pp. 52–53). Increasingly, as repeated throughout this
group of paintings, this backdrop appears both void-like
and associatively related to light and heat—the flicker
of firelight within a cave perhaps. And the bloodied children,
all at once both individual and collective, brownish-red
and white gold, begin likewise to resemble—against this ochre
backdrop—flames, embers, fire: little tongues of heat and
blaze indeed.

On this particular large painting, we see a small boy
standing centrally, dominating the canvas. His body is reddish
brown. He is crying and his face is contorted with pain, hurt,
and anguish. His thin right arm is stretched out, the little
fingers splayed, one raised. His left arm is missing, seemingly
hacked off. His left shoulder is just a stump—some strands of
sinew protruding like ends of red string. On the ground beside
him is what might be a severed hand, but it is adult-sized.
To his left (the viewer's right), just visible, exiting the picture
plane, is what appears to be a younger toddler, apparently
indifferent to the horrific trauma going on behind his back.

The scene is at once harrowing and absurd. Suppose this
were an image from photojournalism? At what point does the
viewer either place a boundary on the deployment of "limit
experience" imagery, and consign its intentions to the morbid,

outdated, and often deluded theories of writers such Georges
Bataille, Maurice Blanchot, or Michel Foucault?

The only answer takes the form of another question:
What then does this painting, these paintings, for all their
shocking violence, propose or confront? Or is their existence
per se a form of anarchism, masked as high aesthetics?
As evidenced by this depiction of a mutilated child, the majority
of the paintings comprising *Fire from the Sun* show a state of
being or society in which the primal is uncontrolled, without
bearings, in a state of anarchy—the id of Freudian primary
process run riot, with no ego to mediate between instinctual
behavior and "reality."

As art-critical shorthand, Freud's definition of the id, from
his *New Introductory Lectures on Psycho-Analysis* (1933),
could double as a summary of *Fire from the Sun*: "It is the dark,
inaccessible part of our personality, what little we know of
it we have learned from our study of the dreamwork and
of course the construction of neurotic symptoms, and most of
that is of a negative character and can be described only
as a contrast to the ego. We approach the id with analogies:
we call it a chaos, a cauldron full of seething excitations. . . .
It is filled with energy reaching it from the instincts, but it
has no organization, produces no collective will, but only
a striving to bring about the satisfaction of the instinctual
needs subject to the observance of the pleasure principle."

As if to illustrate Freud's famous definition, another
painting in the group (p. 55) depicts a (very young) golden-
haired toddler, seen from mid-chest up, looking to one side,
as though his attention had suddenly been caught by some
fresh source of interest. The toddler's stare is absorbed,
concentrated—at once covetous and inquiring. He might have
fallen from a Rococo ceiling, attending God or a gathering
of robed and relaxing gods looking down from a cloud on
a sunburst: a *putto*—chubby, snub-nosed, pretty, with rosy
cheeks, and bow lips. But in this case, the infant's chest
and mouth are messily smeared with "blood"—as though
he had been naughtily gorging himself with jam as opposed,
perhaps, to human flesh.

In two smaller paintings on panel, we see (in the first)
(p. 33), several infants seemingly involved in some kind
of crawling or chasing game: three make their way on
all-fours in a loosely circular manner; another has fallen over;
a fifth child stands to the side, watching, as though hesitant,
his left hand raised to his mouth. The other (p. 7) shows five

children exiting from the center stage, as it were, of where
they have been playing. They look as though they are walking
off set, following a performance.

One little boy looks back; a child in near shadow at the front
seems to be hurrying; at the rear, a little boy seems to stroll
with an accomplished, almost satisfied air. To the viewer's
right, indistinct, just visible, is what seems to be a figure lying
on the floor—possibly adult, possibly not. Behind the departing
children, scattered like abandoned toys, shining, as if greasy
with blood, are what might be sections of body parts or limbs.
There are scuffs, smears, and stains of blood. Beyond the
backdrop, in the foreground of the painting, are what look like
pale old wooden floorboards. The infants seem neither sated
nor tired; rather, that they have been summoned, collectively.

The art of Michaël Borremans seems always to have
been predicated on a confluence of enigma, ambiguity, and
painterly poetics—accosting beauty with strangeness;
making historic romanticism subjugate to mysterious
controlling forces that are neither crudely malevolent nor
necessarily benign. Time and time again in his paintings,
somnambulism and trance appear to be the determining states
of his subjects; they are depicted as though stilled in time,
in darkened or twilit spaces.

Fire from the Sun, as a group of thematically unified
paintings, seems to assert a flagrant intensification of
this vision—aggressively confrontational, indurate, darker,
absurdist almost, balanced between blatant and ambiguous
cruelty. Indifferent to analysis, enigmatic, pre-linguistic,
and seemingly pre-moral, the gory and sinister tableaux
remain open-ended while asserting human nature to be not
only capable of, but founded upon, primal survivalism: vicious,
violent, and voracious.

In this, as in Shakespeare's "Roman" plays or the westerns
of Sergio Leone, their violence and enigma—their hellish
aura, ruddy and ablaze—need not have a meaning, or a goal,
nor be prompted by any notion of straightforward moral
conflict. Like fire, like penumbra, they have no need to be
about anything other than themselves. In some philosophical
dimension or other, they flicker and crackle in a cave.

Fire from the Sun (Two Figures), 2017
Oil on canvas
28 × 32 ¾ inches
71 × 83 cm

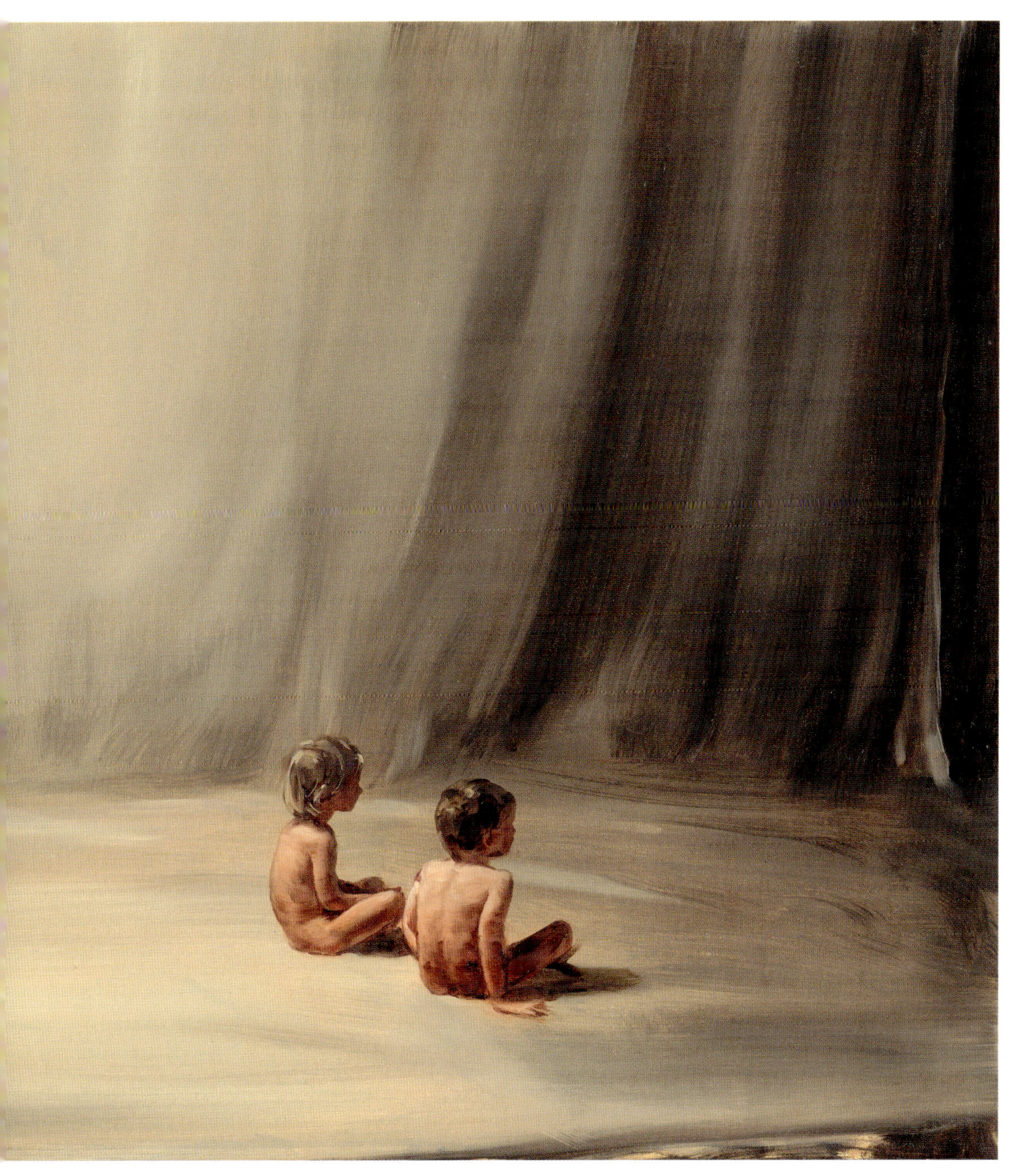

Apparatus, 2017
Oil on canvas
86 ⅝ × 68 ⅞ inches
220 × 175 cm

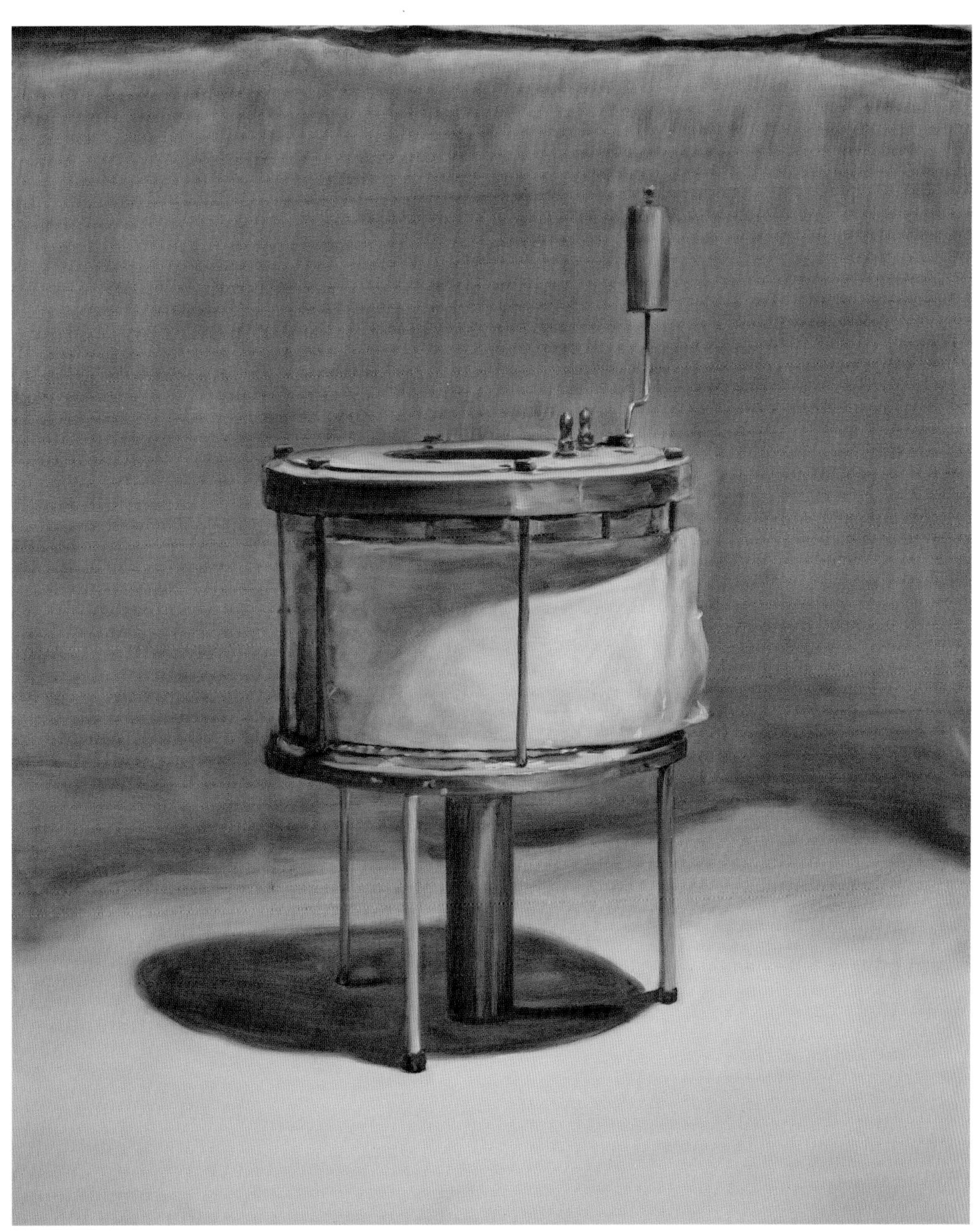

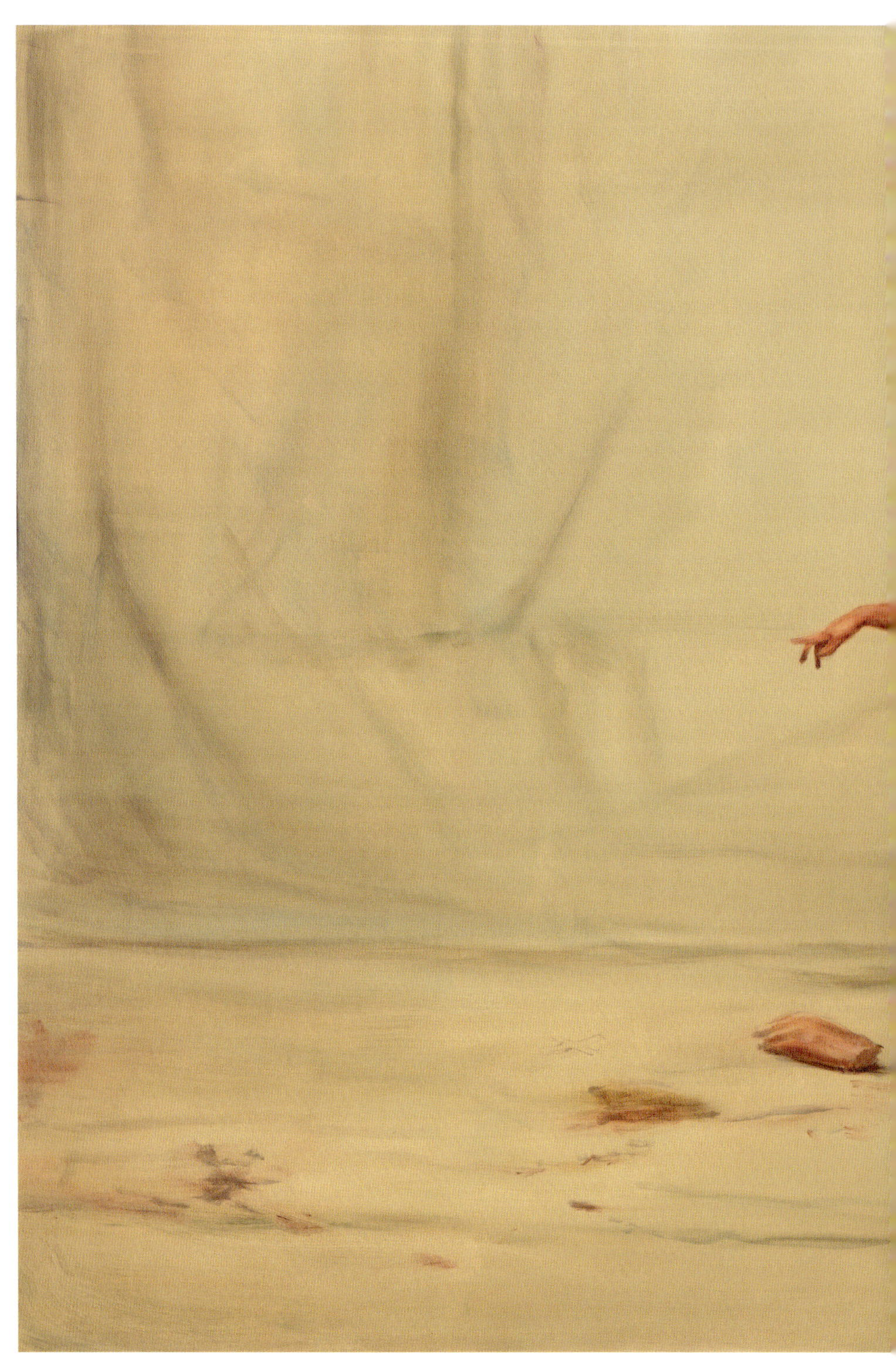

*Fire from the Sun
(Two Figures, One Hand)*, 2017
Oil on canvas
80 ¾ × 110 ¼ inches
205 × 280 cm

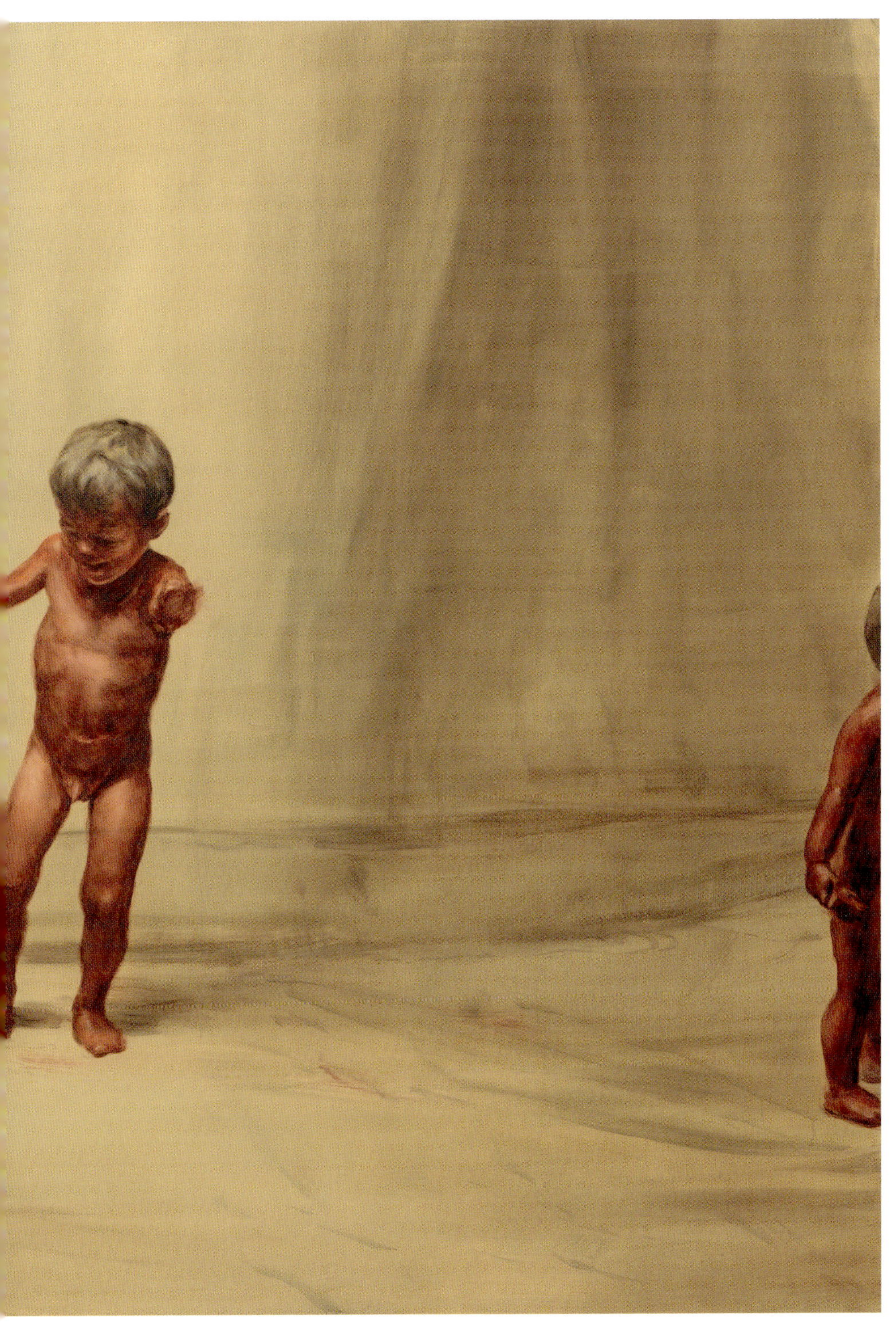

Fire from the Sun, 2017
Oil on panel
11 ½ × 9 ⅞ inches
29.1 × 25.1 cm

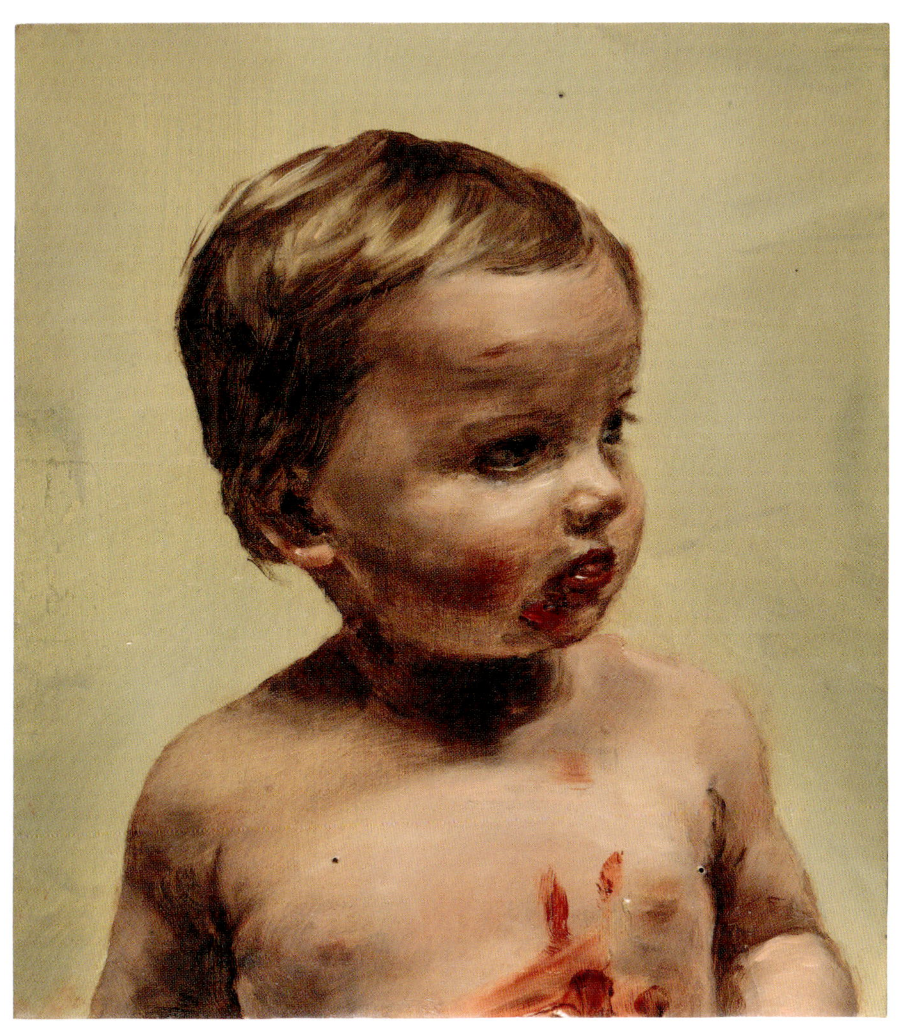

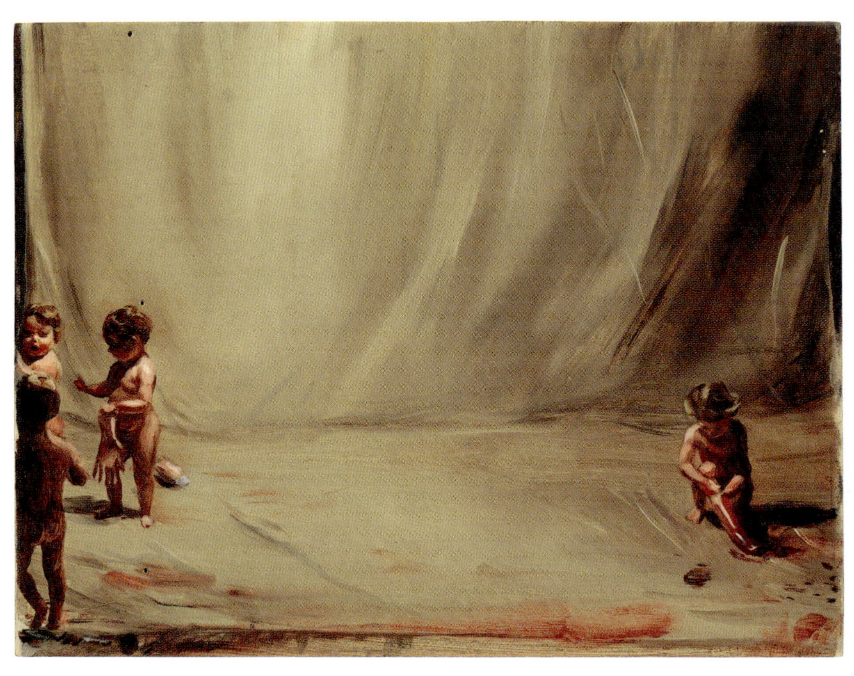

Fire from the Sun, 2017
Oil on panel
9 ½ × 12 ¼ inches
24 × 31 cm

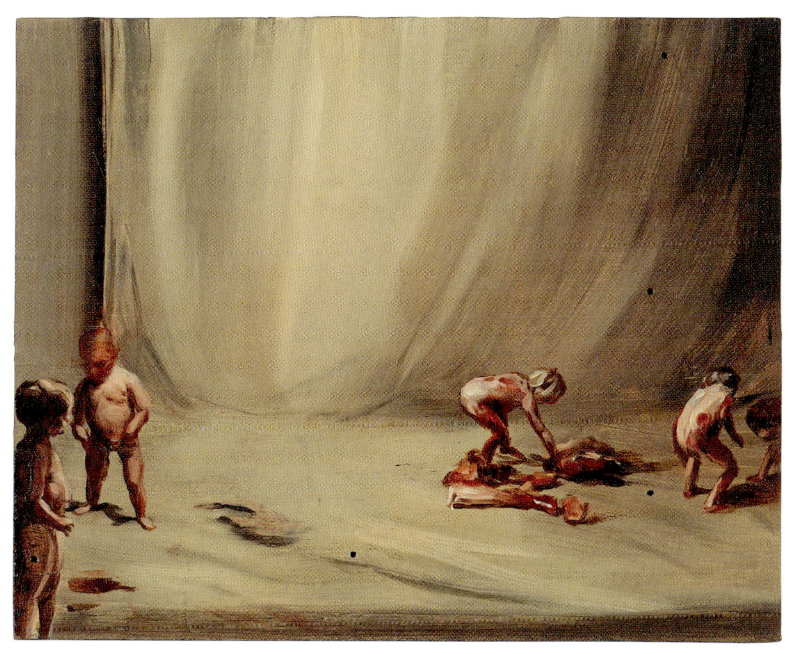

Fire from the Sun, 2017
Oil on panel
8 ¼ × 10 ⅛ inches
21 × 25.7 cm

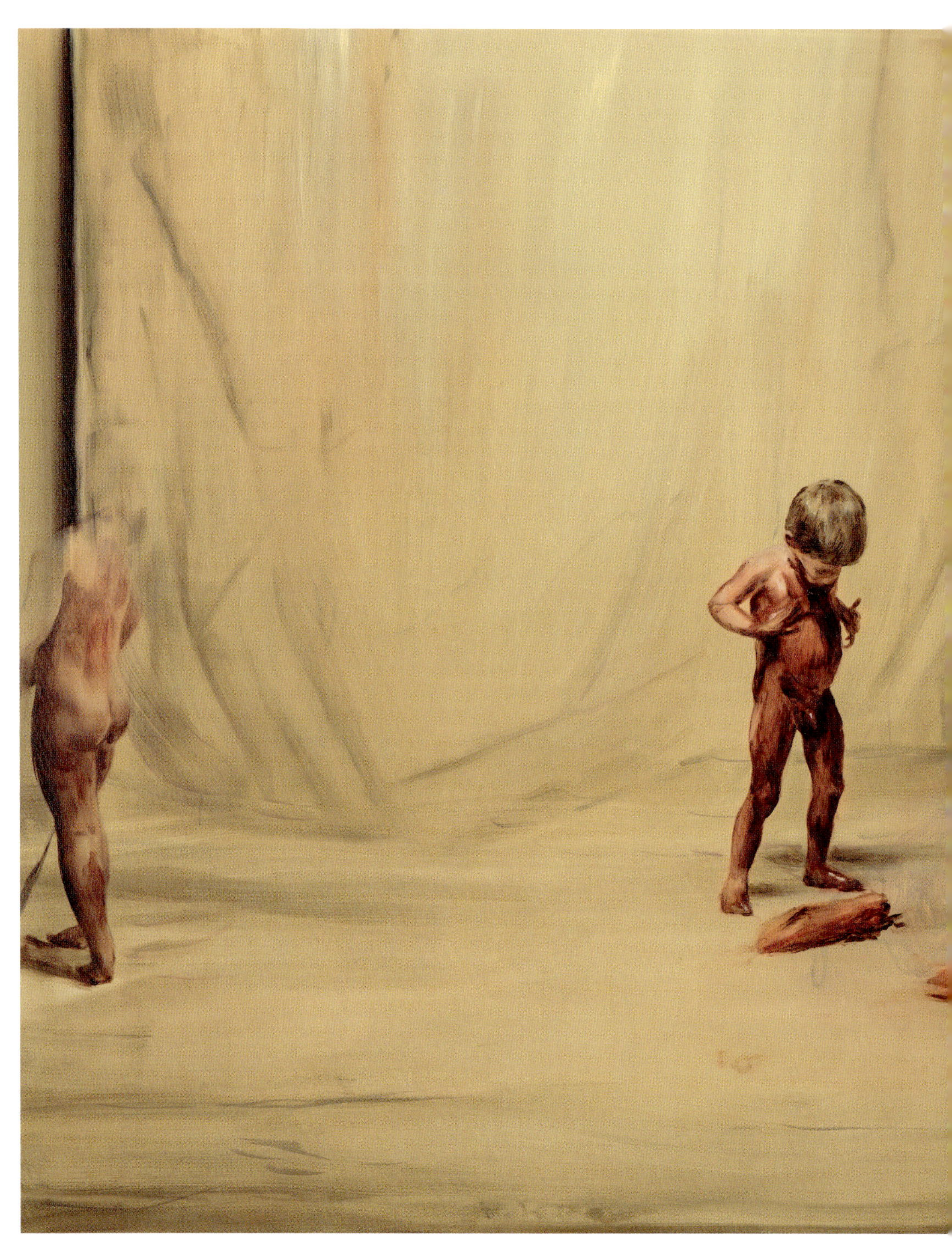

*Fire from the Sun (Five Figures,
Three Limbs)*, 2017
Oil on canvas
74 ⅞ × 118 ⅛ inches
190 × 300 cm

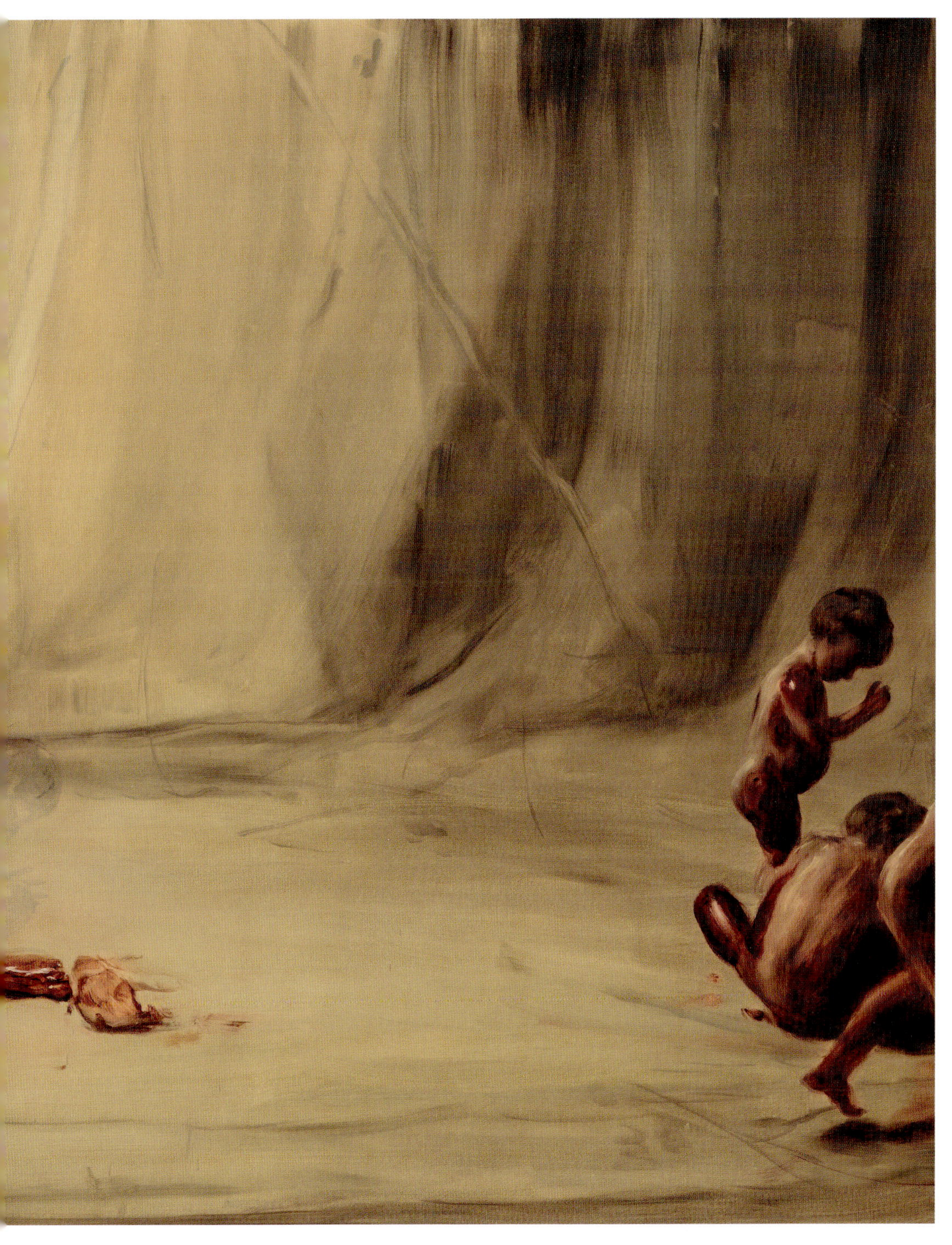

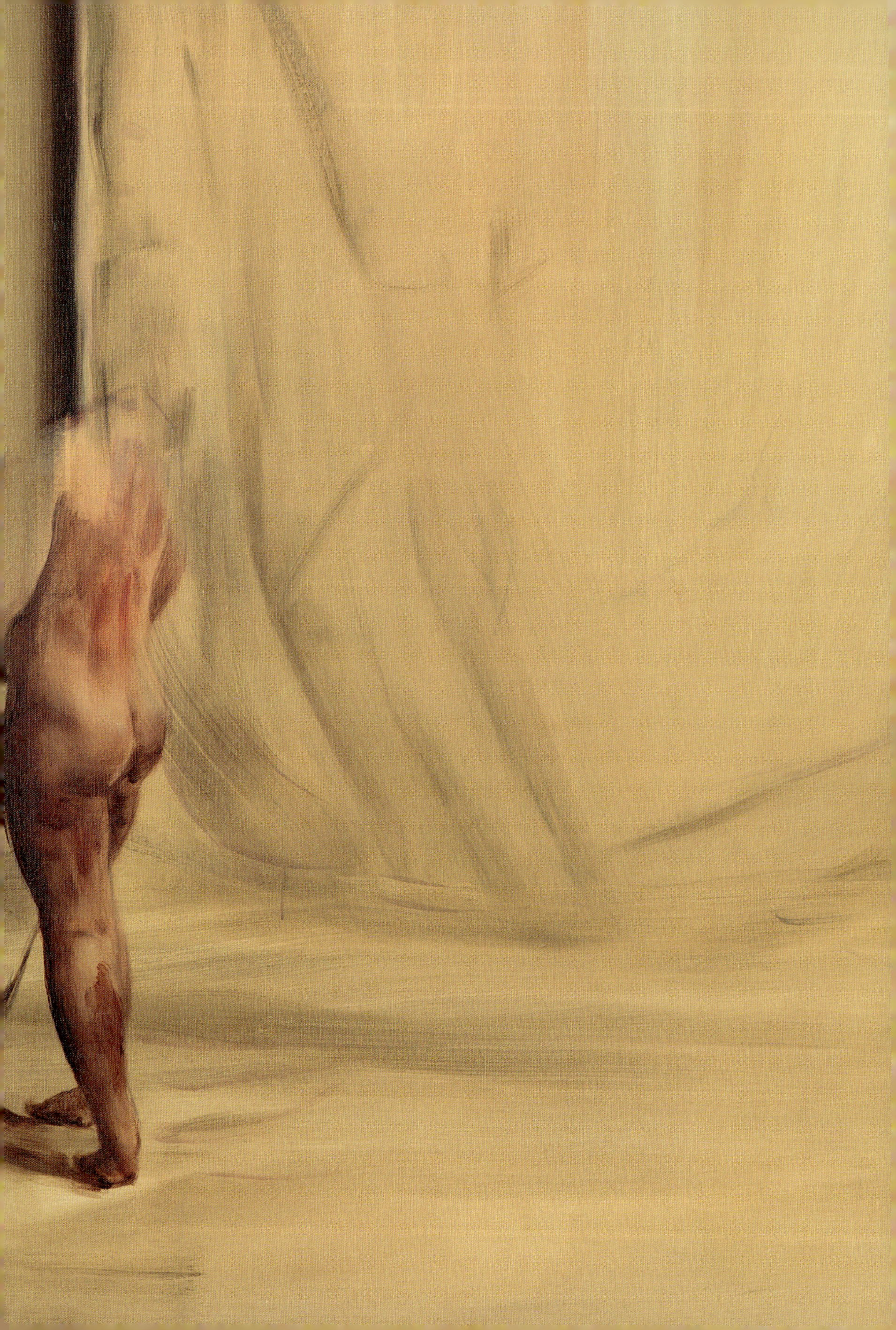

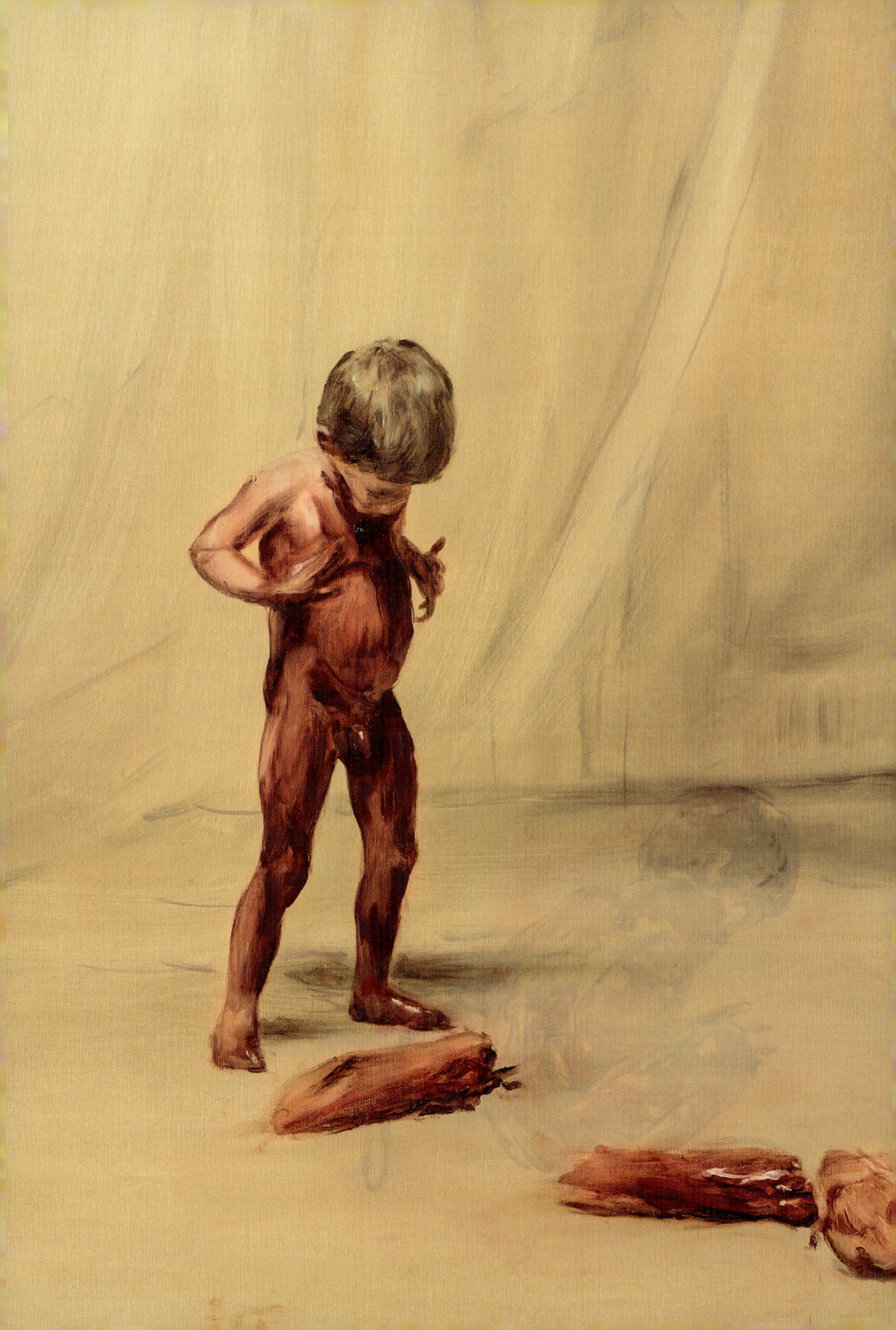

Fire from the Sun, 2017
Oil on cardboard
8 ¼ × 5 ⅞ inches
21 × 14.8 cm

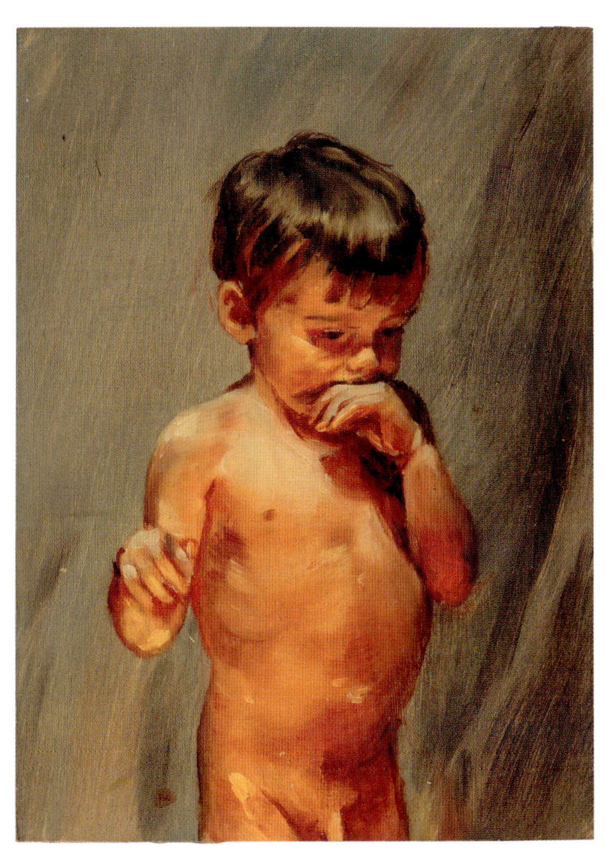

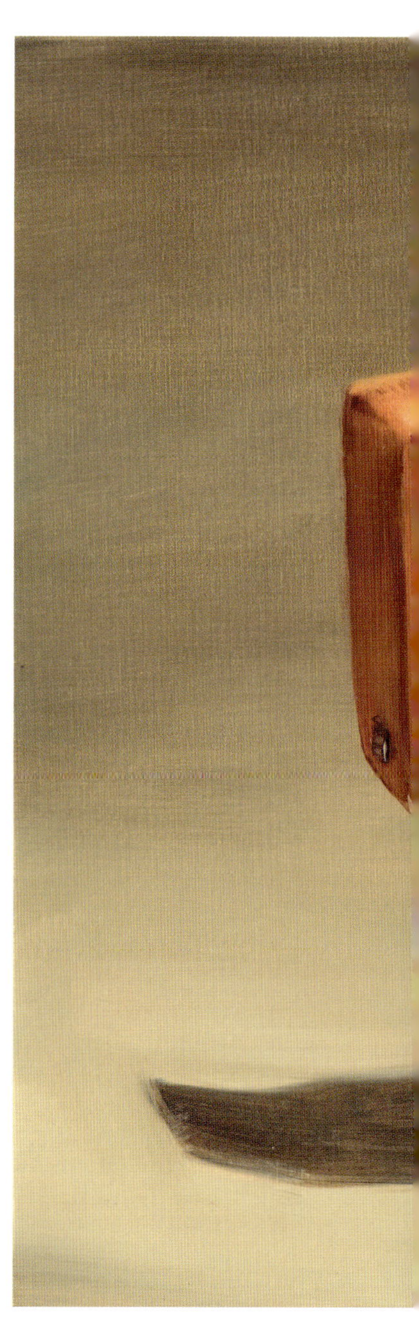

Apparatus (II), 2017
Oil on canvas
25 ⅝ × 32 ⅜ inches
65 × 82 cm

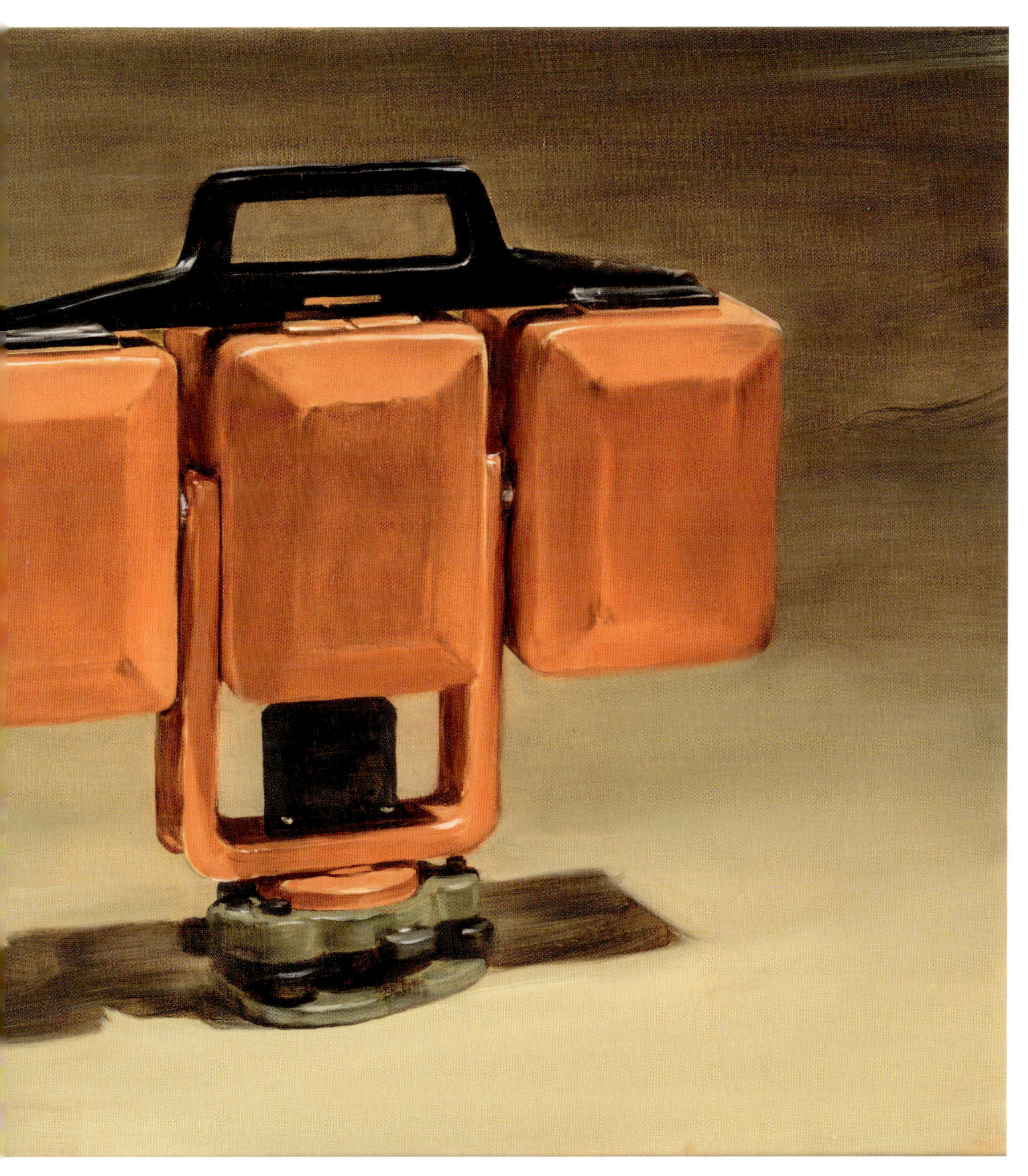

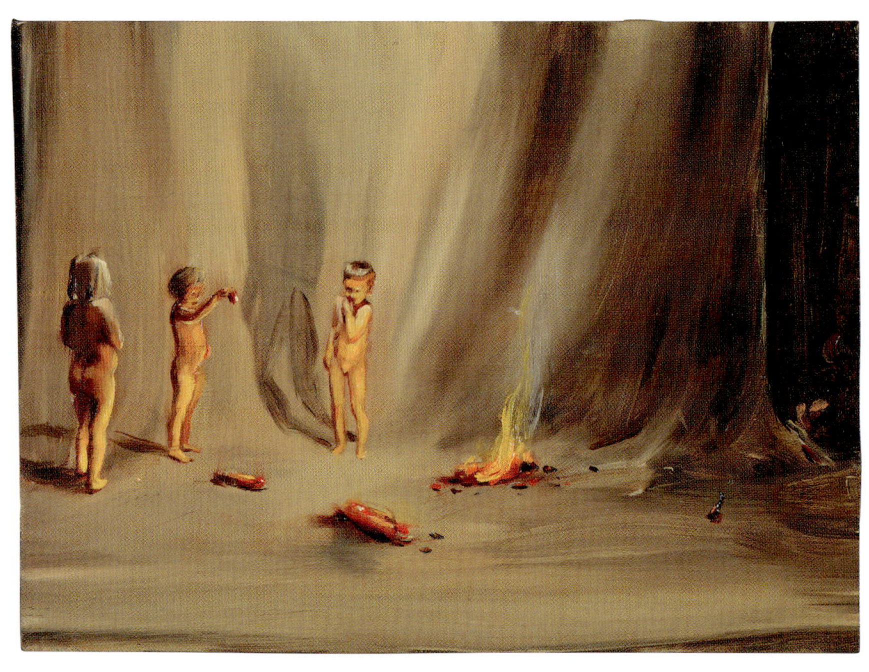

Fire from the Sun, 2017
Oil on panel
8 ⅞ × 11 ¾ inches
22.5 × 29.7 cm

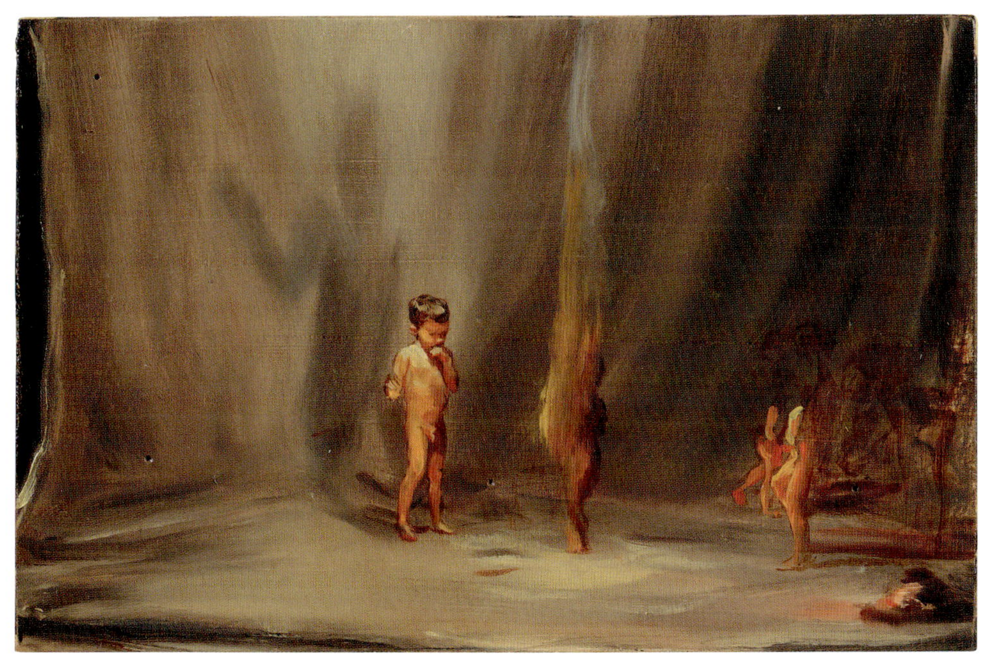

Fire from the Sun, 2017
Oil on panel
8 × 11 ¾ inches
20.2 × 29.8 cm

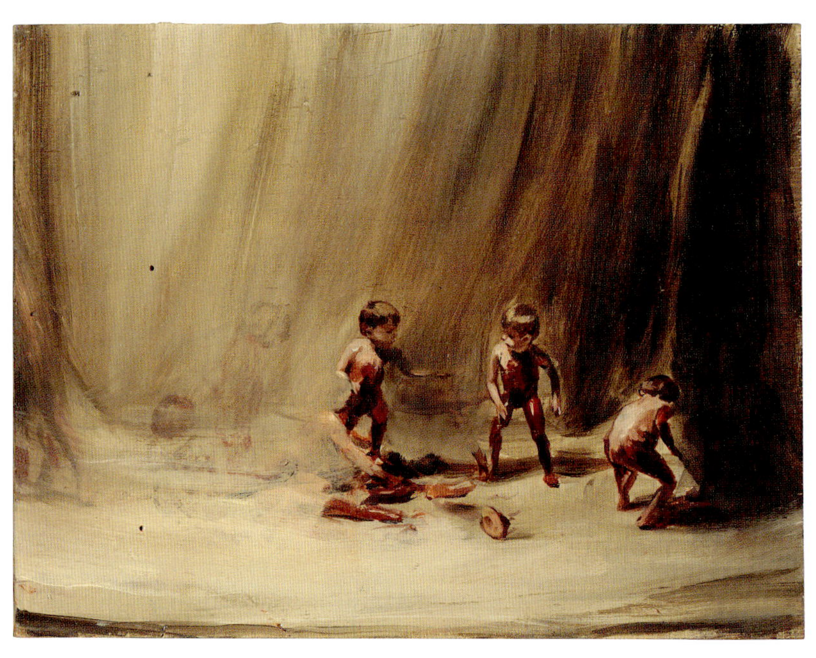

Fire from the Sun, 2017
Oil on panel
9 ⅛ × 11 ⅝ inches
23.1 × 29.3 cm

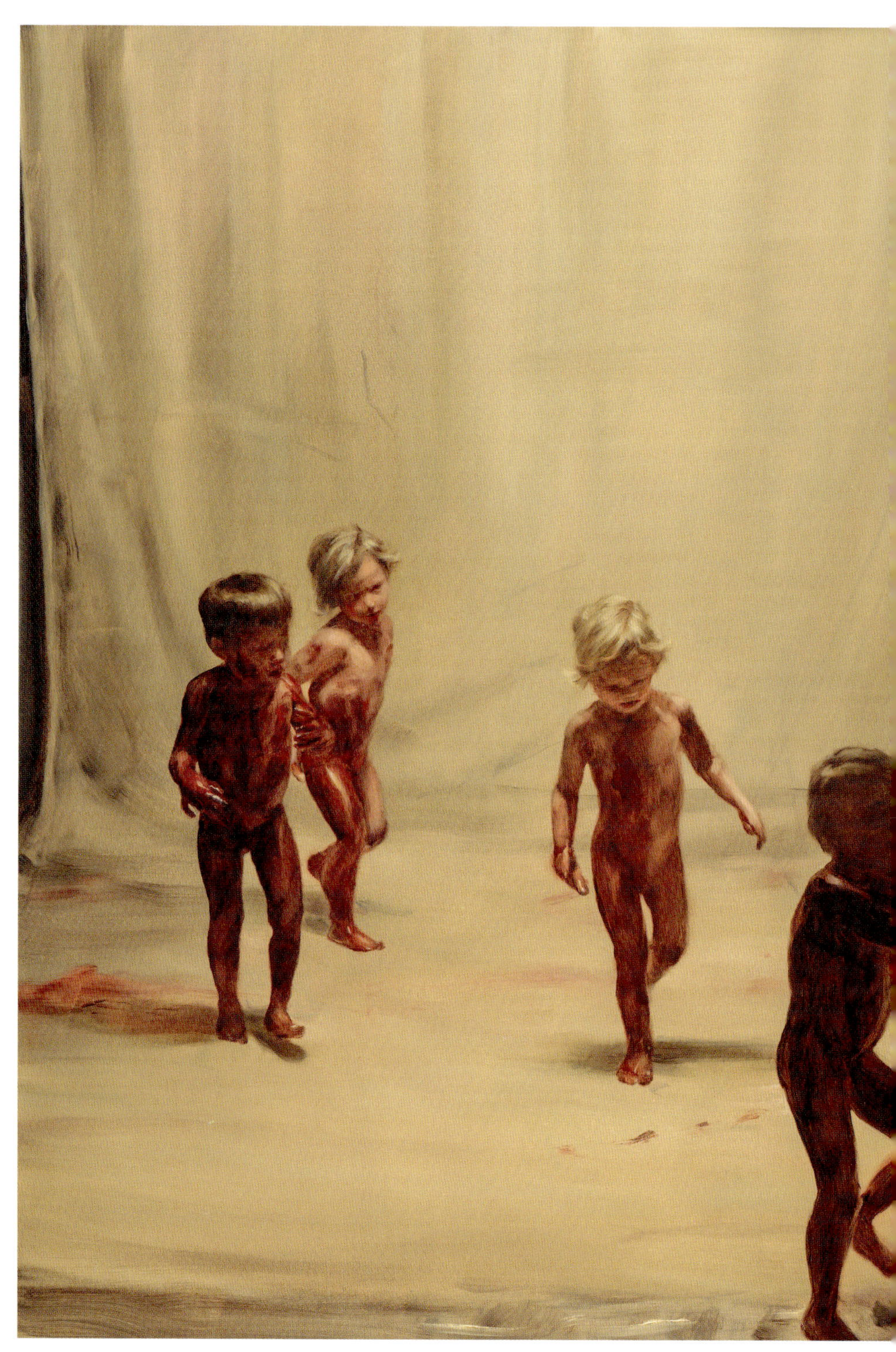

Fire from the Sun (Six Figures,
Three Heads), 2017
Oil on canvas
80 ¾ × 110 ¼ inches
205 × 280 cm

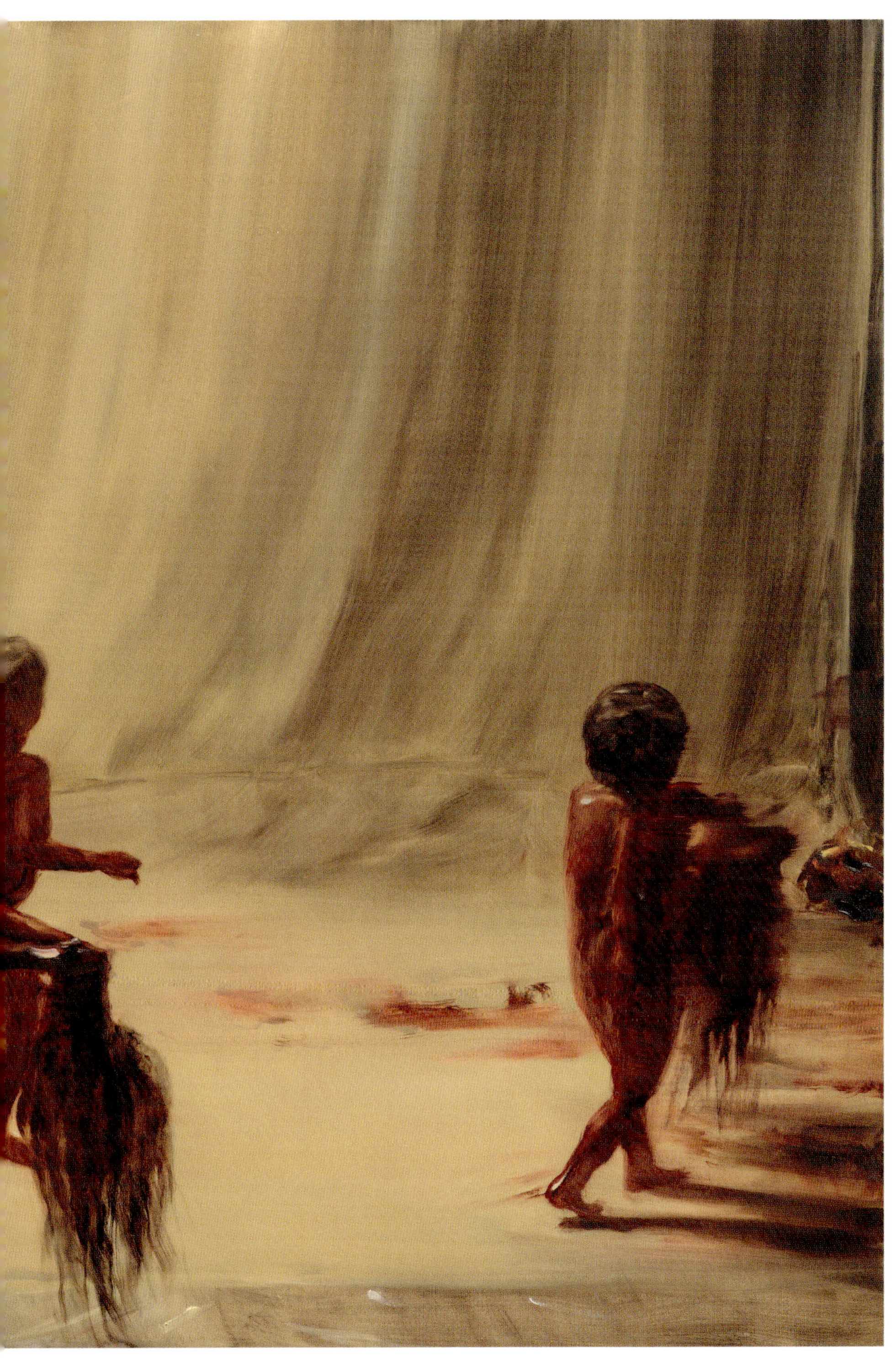

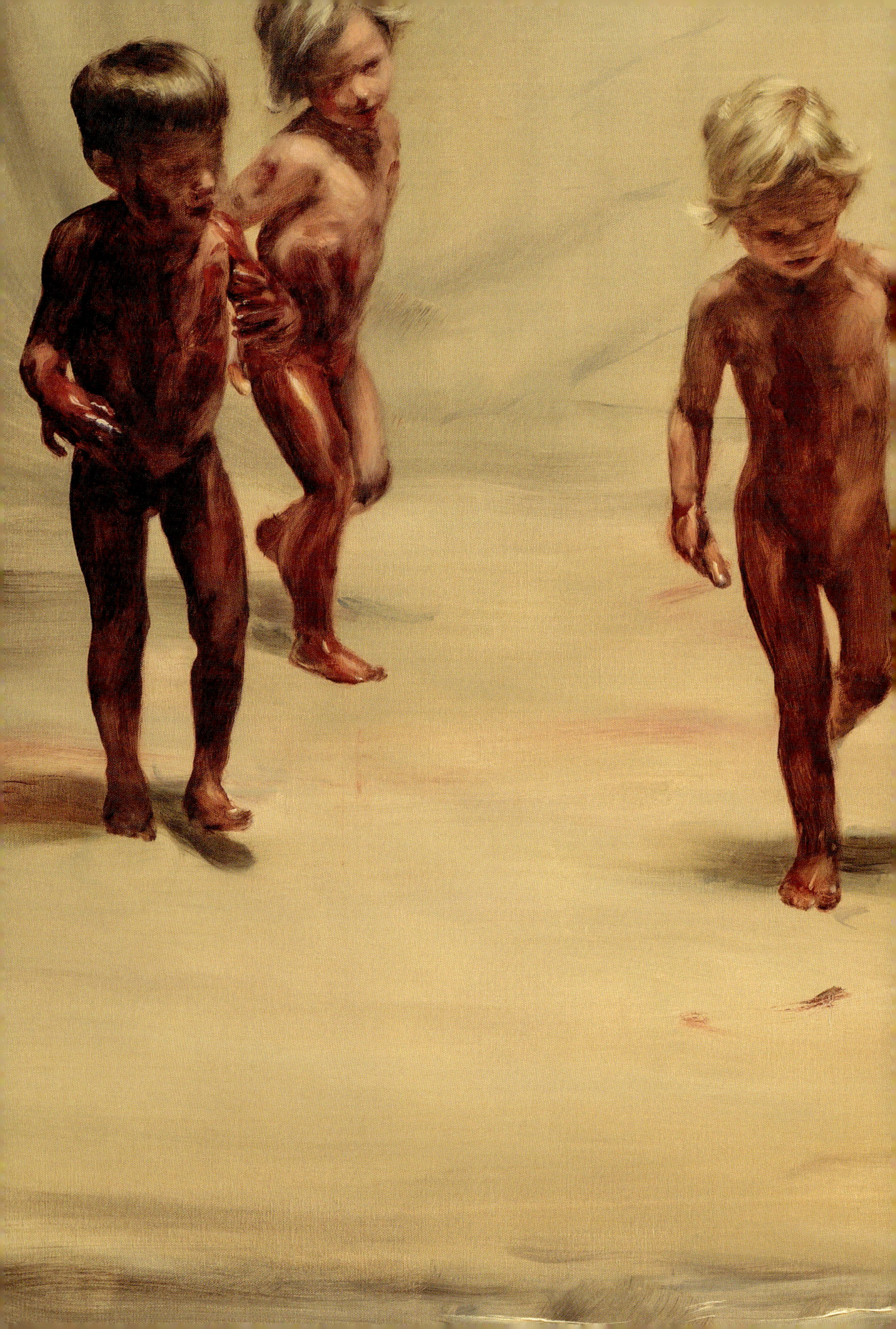

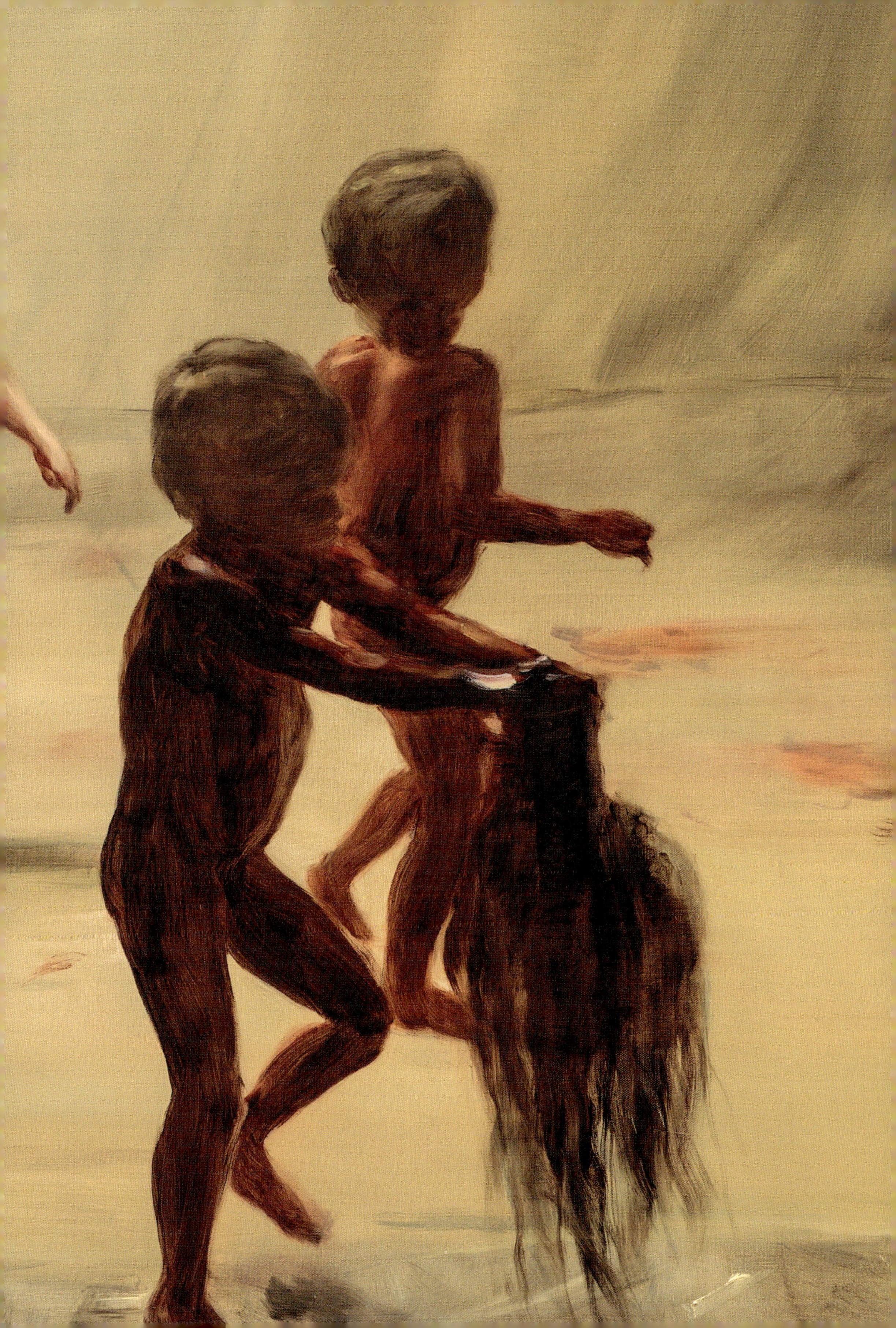

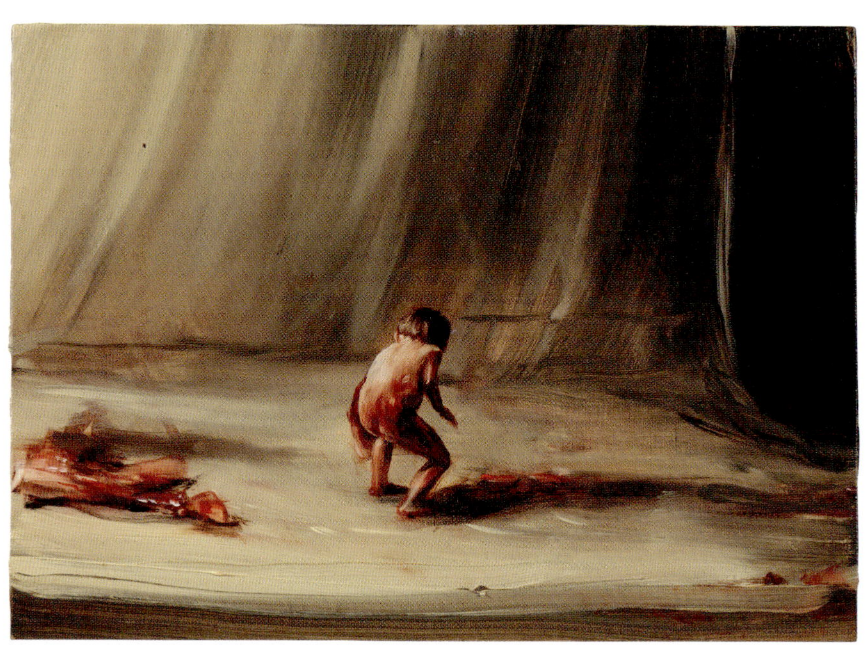

Fire from the Sun, 2017
Oil on panel
9 ⅞ × 13 ⅜ inches
25.1 × 34 cm   75

Fire from the Sun, 2017
Oil on panel
10 ⅜ × 11 ⅝ inches
26.4 × 29.5 cm
Page 5

Fire from the Sun, 2017
Oil on panel
8 ¾ × 12 ¼ inches
22.1 × 31 cm
Page 7

Fire from the Sun, 2017
Oil on panel
10 ¼ × 13 ⅜ inches
26.1 × 34 cm
Page 8

*Fire from the Sun (Three Figures,
One Head, Four Limbs)*, 2017
Oil on canvas
80 ¾ × 110 ¼ inches
205 × 280 cm
Pages 10–11, 12–13, 14–15

Fire from the Sun, 2017
Oil on cardboard
11 ⅛ × 13 ½ inches
28.2 × 34.2 cm
Page 17

Fire from the Sun, 2017
Oil on canvas
17 × 14 ¼ inches
43 × 36 cm
Page 19

Fire from the Sun, 2017
Oil on cardboard
5 ¾ × 8 ¼ inches
14.5 × 21 cm
Page 20

Fire from the Sun, 2017
Oil on cardboard
5 ⅞ × 8 ¼ inches
14.8 × 21 cm
Page 21

*Fire from the Sun (Three Figures,
Two-and-a-Half Limbs)*, 2017
Oil on canvas
80 ¾ × 110 ¼ inches
205 × 280 cm
Pages 22–23, 24–25

*Fire from the Sun (Three Figures,
Three Limbs)*, 2017
Oil on canvas
31 ½ × 41 ⅜ inches
80 × 105 cm
Pages 26–27

Fire from the Sun, 2017
Oil on panel
8 ⅜ × 12 ¼ inches
21.1 × 31 cm
Page 28

Fire from the Sun, 2017
Oil on panel
9 ⅛ × 12 ⅝ inches
23.1 × 32 cm
Page 30

Fire from the Sun, 2017
Oil on panel
8 ⅞ × 12 ⅞ inches
22.5 × 32.7 cm
Page 31

Fire from the Sun, 2017
Oil on canvas on cardboard
9 ⅛ × 14 ⅛ inches
23.1 × 35.9 cm
Page 33

Fire from the Sun, 2017
Oil on panel
8 ⅝ × 10 ⅝ inches
21.7 × 26.9 cm
Page 34

*Fire from the Sun
(Two Figures)*, 2017
Oil on canvas
28 × 32 ¾ inches
71 × 83 cm
Pages 48–49

Apparatus, 2017
Oil on canvas
86 ⅝ × 68 ⅞ inches
220 × 175 cm
Page 51

*Fire from the Sun (Two Figures,
One Hand)*, 2017
Oil on canvas
80 ¾ × 110 ¼ inches
205 × 280 cm
Pages 52–53

Fire from the Sun, 2017
Oil on panel
11 ½ × 9 ⅞ inches
29.1 × 25.1 cm
Page 55

Fire from the Sun, 2017
Oil on panel
9 ½ × 12 ¼ inches
24 × 31 cm
Page 56

Fire from the Sun, 2017
Oil on panel
8 ¼ × 10 ⅛ inches
21 × 25.7 cm
Page 57

*Fire from the Sun (Five Figures,
Three Limbs)*, 2017
Oil on canvas
74 ⅞ × 118 ⅛ inches
190 × 300 cm
Pages 58–59, 60–61

Fire from the Sun, 2017
Oil on cardboard
8 ¼ × 5 ⅞ inches
21 × 14.8 cm
Page 63

Apparatus (II), 2017
Oil on canvas
25 ⅝ × 32 ⅜ inches
65 × 82 cm
Pages 64–65

Fire from the Sun, 2017
Oil on panel
8 ⅞ × 11 ¾ inches
22.5 × 29.7 cm
Page 66

Fire from the Sun, 2017
Oil on panel
8 × 11 ¾ inches
20.2 × 29.8 cm
Page 67

Fire from the Sun, 2017
Oil on panel
9 ⅛ × 11 ⅝ inches
23.1 × 29.3 cm
Page 68

*Fire from the Sun (Six Figures,
Three Heads)*, 2017
Oil on canvas
80 ¾ × 110 ¼ inches
205 × 280 cm
Pages 70–71, 72–73

Fire from the Sun, 2017
Oil on panel
9 ⅞ × 13 ⅜ inches
25.1 × 34 cm
Page 74

David Zwirner wishes to thank Michaël Borremans,
without whom this exhibition and catalogue would not
have been possible, as well as Hanna Schouwink,
Angela Choon, and Kaat DeJonghe. We are especially
grateful to Michael Bracewell for his insightful and
powerful interpretation of Borremans's work.
Additional thanks are extended to Frank Demaegd/Zeno X,
as well as to Paul Au, Janet Chan, Nadia Chan,
Francesca Frediani, Doro Globus, Mary Huber, Hyo Kwon,
Dylan Shuai, Alec Smyth, Molly Stein, Ernest Wan,
Wang Yiquan, Leo Xu, Jennifer Yum, Lucas Zwirner,
Anne Wehr, Chris Wu, and all the staff at David Zwirner,
New York, London, and Hong Kong.

Published by David Zwirner
Books on the occasion of

*Michaël Borremans:
Fire from the Sun*
David Zwirner
5–6/F, H Queen's
80 Queen's Road Central
Central, Hong Kong
January 27–March 10, 2018

David Zwirner Books
529 West 20th Street
2nd Floor
New York, New York 10011
+1 212 727 2070
davidzwirnerbooks.com

Project Managers:
Doro Globus, Lucas Zwirner
Project Editor: Anne Wehr
Project Assistant:
Molly Stein
Proofreader: Dorothy Feaver

Design: Chris Wu,
Hyo Kwon & Janet Chan,
Project Projects, New York
Production Manager:
Paul Au, Gray Balance
Studio Limited
Color Separations:
Gray Balance Studio Limited
Printing: Asia One,
Hong Kong

Typeface: Styrene B
Paper: Arctic Volume White,
150 gsm

Publication © 2018
David Zwirner Books

Text © 2018
Michael Bracewell

All artwork © 2018
Michaël Borremans

Collections
p. 39 (top): Private
Collection; pp. 39 (bottom),
40 (top): Courtesy Zeno
X Gallery, Antwerp; p. 40
(bottom): Private Collection;
p. 41 (top): Private
Collection; p. 41 (bottom):
Qiao Zhibing Collection;
p. 42 (top): Private
Collection; p. 42 (bottom):
Private Collection

Photography
Great care has been
taken to credit all images
correctly. In cases of
errors or omissions, please
contact the publisher
so that corrections can be
made in future editions.
pp. 5, 7, 8, 17, 21, 28, 30, 33,
34, 42 (bottom), 55, 56, 57,
63, 66, 67, 68, 74:
Lieven Herreman
pp. 10–11, 12–13, 14–15, 19,
20, 22–23, 24–25, 26–27,
31, 39 (bottom), 41 (top and
bottom), 42 (top), 48–49,
51, 52–53, 58–59, 60–61,
64–65, 70–71, 72–73:
Peter Cox
p. 39 (top): Dan Bradica
p. 40 (top and bottom):
Ron Amstutz

All rights reserved. No
part of this book may be
reproduced or transmitted
in any form or by any means,
electronic or mechanical,
including photographing,
recording, or information
storage and retrieval,
without prior permission in
writing from the publisher.

Distributed in the United
States and Canada by
ARTBOOK | D.A.P.
75 Broad Street, Suite 630
New York, New York 10004
artbook.com

Distributed outside
the United States
and Canada by
Thames & Hudson, Ltd.
181A High Holborn
London WC1V 7QX
thamesandhudson.com

ISBN 978-1-941701-83-6
LCCN 2017919032

Printed in Hong Kong

Cover: *Fire from the Sun*,
2017 (detail)